EVERYMAN'S LIBRARY

POCKET POETS

Eliot

Poems and Prose

EVERYMAN'S LIBRARY

POCKET POETS

Alfred A. Knopf · New York · Toronto

THIS IS A BORZOI BOOK

PUBLISHED BY ALFRED A. KNOPF, INC.

This selection by Peter Washington first published in
Everyman's Library, 1998
 Published in the United States by Alfred A. Knopf, Inc., New York, and simultaneously in Canada by Random House of Canada Limited, Toronto. Distributed by Random House, Inc., New York

ISBN 0-375-40185-7

Typography by Peter B. Willberg

Typeset in the UK by AccComputing, Castle Cary, Somerset

Printed in Great Britain at Mackays of Chatham PLC
by arrangement with Associated Agencies Ltd.

T. S. ELIOT

CONTENTS

PRUFROCK

AND OTHER

OBSERVATIONS

For Jean Verdenal, 1889–1915
mort aux Dardanelles

Or puoi la quantitate
comprender dell'amor ch'a te mi scalda,
quando dismento nostra vanitate,
trattando l'ombre come cosa salda.

THE LOVE SONG OF J. ALFRED PRUFROCK

S'io credessi che mia risposta fosse
a persona che mai tornasse al mondo,
questa fiamma staria senza più scosse.
Ma per ciò che giammai di questo fondo
non tornò vivo alcun, s'i'odo il vero,
senza tema d'infamia ti rispondo.

Let us go then, you and I,
When the evening is spread out against the sky
Like a patient etherised upon a table;
Let us go, through certain half-deserted streets,
The muttering retreats
Of restless nights in one-night cheap hotels
And sawdust restaurants with oyster-shells:
Streets that follow like a tedious argument
Of insidious intent
To lead you to an overwhelming question . . .
Oh, do not ask, 'What is it?'
Let us go and make our visit.

In the room the women come and go
Talking of Michelangelo.

The yellow fog that rubs its back upon the window-panes,
The yellow smoke that rubs its muzzle on the window-panes,
Licked its tongue into the corners of the evening,
Lingered upon the pools that stand in drains,
Let fall upon its back the soot that falls from chimneys,
Slipped by the terrace, made a sudden leap,
And seeing that it was a soft October night,
Curled once about the house, and fell asleep.

And indeed there will be time
For the yellow smoke that slides along the street
Rubbing its back upon the window-panes;
There will be time, there will be time
To prepare a face to meet the faces that you meet;
There will be time to murder and create,
And time for all the works and days of hands
That lift and drop a question on your plate;
Time for you and time for me,
And time yet for a hundred indecisions,
And for a hundred visions and revisions,
Before the taking of a toast and tea.

In the room the women come and go
Talking of Michelangelo.

And indeed there will be time
To wonder, 'Do I dare?' and, 'Do I dare?'
Time to turn back and descend the stair,
With a bald spot in the middle of my hair—
(They will say: 'How his hair is growing thin!')
My morning coat, my collar mounting firmly
to the chin,
My necktie rich and modest, but asserted by a
simple pin—
(They will say: 'But how his arms and legs are thin!')
Do I dare
Disturb the universe?
In a minute there is time
For decisions and revisions which a minute
will reverse.

For I have known them all already, known
them all—
Have known the evenings, mornings, afternoons,
I have measured out my life with coffee spoons;
I know the voices dying with a dying fall
Beneath the music from a farther room.
So how should I presume?

And I have known the eyes already, known
them all—
The eyes that fix you in a formulated phrase,

And when I am formulated, sprawling on a pin,
When I am pinned and wriggling on the wall,
Then how should I begin
To spit out all the butt-ends of my days and ways?
    And how should I presume?

    And I have known the arms already, known
        them all—
Arms that are braceleted and white and bare
(But in the lamplight, downed with light brown hair!)
Is it perfume from a dress
That makes me so digress?
Arms that lie along a table, or wrap about a shawl.
    And should I then presume?
    And how should I begin?

* * *

    Shall I say, I have gone at dusk through narrow
        streets
And watched the smoke that rises from the pipes
Of lonely men in shirt-sleeves, leaning out of
        windows? . . .

    I should have been a pair of ragged claws
Scuttling across the floors of silent seas.

* * *

And the afternoon, the evening, sleeps so peacefully!
Smoothed by long fingers,
Asleep . . . tired . . . or it malingers,
Stretched on the floor, here beside you and me.
Should I, after tea and cakes and ices,
Have the strength to force the moment to its crisis?
But though I have wept and fasted, wept and prayed,
Though I have seen my head (grown slightly bald) brought in upon a platter,
I am no prophet—and here's no great matter;
I have seen the moment of my greatness flicker,
And I have seen the eternal Footman hold my coat, and snicker,
And in short, I was afraid.

And would it have been worth it, after all,
After the cups, the marmalade, the tea,
Among the porcelain, among some talk of you and me,
Would it have been worth while,
To have bitten off the matter with a smile,
To have squeezed the universe into a ball
To roll it towards some overwhelming question,
To say: 'I am Lazarus, come from the dead,
Come back to tell you all, I shall tell you all'—
If one, settling a pillow by her head,
Should say: 'That is not what I meant at all.
That is not it, at all.'

And would it have been worth it, after all,
Would it have been worth while,
After the sunsets and the dooryards and the sprinkled streets,
After the novels, after the teacups, after the skirts that trail along the floor—
And this, and so much more?—
It is impossible to say just what I mean!
But as if a magic lantern threw the nerves in patterns on a screen:
Would it have been worth while
If one, settling a pillow or throwing off a shawl,
And turning toward the window, should say:
'That is not it at all,
That is not what I meant at all.'

* * *

No! I am not Prince Hamlet, nor was meant to be;
Am an attendant lord, one that will do
To swell a progress, start a scene or two,
Advise the prince; no doubt, an easy tool,
Deferential, glad to be of use,
Politic, cautious, and meticulous;
Full of high sentence, but a bit obtuse;
At times, indeed, almost ridiculous—
Almost, at times, the Fool.

I grow old . . . I grow old . . .
I shall wear the bottoms of my trousers rolled.

Shall I part my hair behind? Do I dare to eat
a peach?
I shall wear white flannel trousers, and walk upon
the beach.
I have heard the mermaids singing, each to each.

I do not think that they will sing to me.

I have seen them riding seaward on the waves
Combing the white hair of the waves blown back
When the wind blows the water white and black.

We have lingered in the chambers of the sea
By sea-girls wreathed with seaweed red and brown
Till human voices wake us, and we drown.

PORTRAIT OF A LADY

Thou hast committed—
Fornication: but that was in another country,
And besides, the wench is dead.

The Jew of Malta

I

Among the smoke and fog of a December afternoon
You have the scene arrange itself—as it will seem
to do—
With 'I have saved this afternoon for you';
And four wax candles in the darkened room,
Four rings of light upon the ceiling overhead,
An atmosphere of Juliet's tomb
Prepared for all the things to be said, or left unsaid.
We have been, let us say, to hear the latest Pole
Transmit the Preludes, through his hair and
finger-tips.
'So intimate, this Chopin, that I think his soul
Should be resurrected only among friends
Some two or three, who will not touch the bloom
That is rubbed and questioned in the concert room.'
—And so the conversation slips
Among velleities and carefully caught regrets
Through attenuated tones of violins
Mingled with remote cornets

And begins.
'You do not know how much they mean to me,
    my friends,
And how, how rare and strange it is, to find
In a life composed so much, so much of odds and ends,
(For indeed I do not love it . . . you knew? you are
    not blind!
How keen you are!)
To find a friend who has these qualities,
Who has, and gives
Those qualities upon which friendship lives.
How much it means that I say this to you—
Without these friendships—life, what *cauchemar!*'

Among the windings of the violins
And the ariettes
Of cracked cornets
Inside my brain a dull tom-tom begins
Absurdly hammering a prelude of its own,
Capricious monotone
That is at least one definite 'false note.'
—Let us take the air, in a tobacco trance,
Admire the monuments,
Discuss the late events,
Correct our watches by the public clocks.
Then sit for half an hour and drink our bocks.

II

Now that lilacs are in bloom
She has a bowl of lilacs in her room
And twists one in her fingers while she talks.
'Ah, my friend, you do not know, you do not know
What life is, you who hold it in your hands';
(Slowly twisting the lilac stalks)
'You let it flow from you, you let it flow,
And youth is cruel, and has no more remorse
And smiles at situations which it cannot see.'
I smile, of course,
And go on drinking tea.

'Yet with these April sunsets, that somehow recall
My buried life, and Paris in the Spring,
I feel immeasurably at peace, and find the world
To be wonderful and youthful, after all.'

The voice returns like the insistent out-of-tune
Of a broken violin on an August afternoon:
'I am always sure that you understand
My feelings, always sure that you feel,
Sure that across the gulf you reach your hand.

You are invulnerable, you have no Achilles' heel.
You will go on, and when you have prevailed
You can say: at this point many a one has failed.

But what have I, but what have I, my friend,
To give you, what can you receive from me?
Only the friendship and the sympathy
Of one about to reach her journey's end.

I shall sit here, serving tea to friends. . . .'

I take my hat: how can I make a cowardly amends
For what she has said to me?
You will see me any morning in the park
Reading the comics and the sporting page.
Particularly I remark
An English countess goes upon the stage.
A Greek was murdered at a Polish dance,
Another bank defaulter has confessed.
I keep my countenance,
I remain self-possessed
Except when a street-piano, mechanical and tired
Reiterates some worn-out common song
With the smell of hyacinths across the garden
Recalling things that other people have desired.
Are these ideas right or wrong?

III

The October night comes down: returning as before
Except for a slight sensation of being ill at ease
I mount the stairs and turn the handle of the door

And feel as if I had mounted on my hands and knees.
'And so you are going abroad; and when do you return?
But that's a useless question.
You hardly know when you are coming back,
You will find so much to learn.'
My smile falls heavily among the bric-à-brac.

'Perhaps you can write to me.'
My self-possession flares up for a second;
This is as I had reckoned.
'I have been wondering frequently of late
(But our beginnings never know our ends!)
Why we have not developed into friends.'
I feel like one who smiles, and turning shall remark
Suddenly, his expression in a glass.
My self-possession gutters; we are really in the dark.

'For everybody said so, all our friends,
They all were sure our feelings would relate
So closely! I myself can hardly understand.
We must leave it now to fate.
You will write, at any rate.
Perhaps it is not too late.
I shall sit here, serving tea to friends.'

And I must borrow every changing shape
To find expression . . . dance, dance

Like a dancing bear,
Cry like a parrot, chatter like an ape.
Let us take the air, in a tobacco trance—

Well! and what if she should die some afternoon,
Afternoon grey and smoky, evening yellow and rose;
Should die and leave me sitting pen in hand
With the smoke coming down above the housetops;
Doubtful, for a while
Not knowing what to feel or if I understand
Or whether wise or foolish, tardy or too soon . . .
Would she not have the advantage, after all?
This music is successful with a 'dying fall'
Now that we talk of dying—
And should I have the right to smile?

PRELUDES

I

The winter evening settles down
With smell of steaks in passageways.
Six o'clock.
The burnt-out ends of smoky days.
And now a gusty shower wraps
The grimy scraps
Of withered leaves about your feet
And newspapers from vacant lots;
The showers beat
On broken blinds and chimney-pots,
And at the corner of the street
A lonely cab-horse steams and stamps.

And then the lighting of the lamps.

II

The morning comes to consciousness
Of faint stale smells of beer
From the sawdust-trampled street
With all its muddy feet that press
To early coffee-stands.

With the other masquerades
That time resumes,

One thinks of all the hands
That are raising dingy shades
In a thousand furnished rooms.

III

You tossed a blanket from the bed,
You lay upon your back, and waited;
You dozed, and watched the night revealing
The thousand sordid images
Of which your soul was constituted;
They flickered against the ceiling.
And when all the world came back
And the light crept up between the shutters,
And you heard the sparrows in the gutters,
You had such a vision of the street
As the street hardly understands;
Sitting along the bed's edge, where
You curled the papers from your hair,
Or clasped the yellow soles of feet
In the palms of both soiled hands.

IV

His soul stretched tight across the skies
That fade behind a city block,
Or trampled by insistent feet
At four and five and six o'clock;
And short square fingers stuffing pipes,

And evening newspapers, and eyes
Assured of certain certainties,
The conscience of a blackened street
Impatient to assume the world.

I am moved by fancies that are curled
Around these images, and cling:
The notion of some infinitely gentle
Infinitely suffering thing.

Wipe your hand across your mouth, and laugh;
The worlds revolve like ancient women
Gathering fuel in vacant lots.

RHAPSODY ON A WINDY NIGHT

Twelve o'clock.
Along the reaches of the street
Held in a lunar synthesis,
Whispering lunar incantations
Dissolve the floors of memory
And all its clear relations,
Its divisions and precisions.
Every street-lamp that I pass
Beats like a fatalistic drum,
And through the spaces of the dark
Midnight shakes the memory
As a madman shakes a dead geranium.

Half-past one,
The street-lamp sputtered,
The street-lamp muttered,
The street-lamp said, 'Regard that woman
Who hesitates toward you in the light of the door
Which opens on her like a grin.
You see the border of her dress
Is torn and stained with sand,
And you see the corner of her eye
Twists like a crooked pin.'

The memory throws up high and dry
A crowd of twisted things;
A twisted branch upon the beach
Eaten smooth, and polished
As if the world gave up
The secret of its skeleton,
Stiff and white.
A broken spring in a factory yard,
Rust that clings to the form that the strength has left
Hard and curled and ready to snap.

Half-past two,
The street-lamp said,
'Remark the cat which flattens itself in the gutter,
Slips out its tongue
And devours a morsel of rancid butter.'
So the hand of the child, automatic,
Slipped out and pocketed a toy that was running along
    the quay.
I could see nothing behind that child's eye.
I have seen eyes in the street
Trying to peer through lighted shutters,
And a crab one afternoon in a pool,
An old crab with barnacles on his back,
Gripped the end of a stick which I held him.

Half-past three,
The lamp sputtered,
The lamp muttered in the dark.
The lamp hummed:
'Regard the moon,
La lune ne garde aucune rancune,
She winks a feeble eye,
She smiles into corners.
She smooths the hair of the grass.
The moon has lost her memory.
A washed-out smallpox cracks her face,

Her hand twists a paper rose,
That smells of dust and eau de Cologne,
She is alone
With all the old nocturnal smells
That cross and cross across her brain.'
The reminiscence comes
Of sunless dry geraniums
And dust in crevices,
Smells of chestnuts in the streets,
And female smells in shuttered rooms,
And cigarettes in corridors
And cocktail smells in bars.

The lamp said,
'Four o'clock,

Here is the number on the door.
Memory!
You have the key,
The little lamp spreads a ring on the stair.
Mount.
The bed is open; the tooth-brush hangs on the wall,
Put your shoes at the door, sleep, prepare for life.'

The last twist of the knife.

MORNING AT THE WINDOW

They are rattling breakfast plates in basement
    kitchens,
And along the trampled edges of the street
I am aware of the damp souls of housemaids
Sprouting despondently at area gates.

The brown waves of fog toss up to me
Twisted faces from the bottom of the street,
And tear from a passer-by with muddy skirts
An aimless smile that hovers in the air
And vanishes along the level of the roofs.

THE *'BOSTON EVENING TRANSCRIPT'*

The readers of the *Boston Evening Transcript*
Sway in the wind like a field of ripe corn.

When evening quickens faintly in the street,
Wakening the appetites of life in some
And to others bringing the *Boston Evening Transcript*,
I mount the steps and ring the bell, turning
Wearily, as one would turn to nod good-bye to
    La Rochefoucauld,
If the street were time and he at the end of the street,
And I say, 'Cousin Harriet, here is the *Boston Evening*
    Transcript.'

AUNT HELEN

Miss Helen Slingsby was my maiden aunt,
And lived in a small house near a fashionable square
Cared for by servants to the number of four.
Now when she died there was silence in heaven
And silence at her end of the street.
The shutters were drawn and the undertaker wiped
his feet—
He was aware that this sort of thing had occurred
before.
The dogs were handsomely provided for,
But shortly afterwards the parrot died too.
The Dresden clock continued ticking on the
mantelpiece,
And the footman sat upon the dining-table
Holding the second housemaid on his knees—
Who had always been so careful while her mistress
lived.

COUSIN NANCY

Miss Nancy Ellicott
Strode across the hills and broke them,
Rode across the hills and broke them—
The barren New England hills—
Riding to hounds
Over the cow-pasture.

Miss Nancy Ellicott smoked
And danced all the modern dances;
And her aunts were not quite sure how they
    felt about it,
But they knew that it was modern.

Upon the glazen shelves kept watch
Matthew and Waldo, guardians of the faith,
The army of unalterable law.

MR APOLLINAX

Ω τῆς καινότητος. Ἡράκλεις, τῆς παραδοξολογίας.
εὐμήχανος ἄνθρωπος.

LUCIAN

When Mr Apollinax visited the United States
His laughter tinkled among the teacups.
I thought of Fragilion, that shy figure among the
birch-trees,
And of Priapus in the shrubbery
Gaping at the lady in the swing.
In the palace of Mrs Phlaccus, at Professor Channing-
Cheetah's
He laughed like an irresponsible foetus.
His laughter was submarine and profound
Like the old man of the sea's
Hidden under coral islands
Where worried bodies of drowned men drift down
in the green silence,
Dropping from fingers of surf.

I looked for the head of Mr Apollinax rolling
under a chair
Or grinning over a screen
With seaweed in its hair.
I heard the beat of centaur's hoofs over the hard turf

As his dry and passionate talk devoured the afternoon.
'He is a charming man'—'But after all what did he
mean?'—
'His pointed ears. . . . He must be unbalanced.'—
'There was something he said that I might have
challenged.'
Of dowager Mrs Phlaccus, and Professor and
Mrs Cheetah
I remember a slice of lemon, and a bitten macaroon.

HYSTERIA

As she laughed I was aware of becoming involved in her laughter and being part of it, until her teeth were only accidental stars with a talent for squad-drill. I was drawn in by short gasps, inhaled at each momentary recovery, lost finally in the dark caverns of her throat, bruised by the ripple of unseen muscles. An elderly waiter with trembling hands was hurriedly spreading a pink and white checked cloth over the rusty green iron table, saying: 'If the lady and gentleman wish to take their tea in the garden, if the lady and gentleman wish to take their tea in the garden...' I decided that if the shaking of her breasts could be stopped, some of the fragments of the afternoon might be collected, and I concentrated my attention with careful subtlety to this end.

CONVERSATION GALANTE

I observe: 'Our sentimental friend the moon!
Or possibly (fantastic, I confess)
It may be Prester John's balloon
Or an old battered lantern hung aloft
To light poor travellers to their distress.'
  She then: 'How you digress!'

And I then: 'Someone frames upon the keys
That exquisite nocturne, with which we explain
The night and moonshine; music which we seize
To body forth our own vacuity.'
  She then: 'Does this refer to me?'
  'Oh no, it is I who am inane.'

'You, madam, are the eternal humorist,
The eternal enemy of the absolute,
Giving our vagrant moods the slightest twist!
With your air indifferent and imperious
At a stroke our mad poetics to confute—'
  And—'Are we then so serious?'

LA FIGLIA CHE PIANGE

O quam te memorem virgo . . .

Stand on the highest pavement of the stair—
Lean on a garden urn—
Weave, weave the sunlight in your hair—
Clasp your flowers to you with a pained surprise—
Fling them to the ground and turn
With a fugitive resentment in your eyes:
But weave, weave the sunlight in your hair.

So I would have had him leave,
So I would have had her stand and grieve,
So he would have left
As the soul leaves the body torn and bruised,
As the mind deserts the body it has used.
I should find
Some way incomparably light and deft,
Some way we both should understand,
Simple and faithless as a smile and shake of the hand.

She turned away, but with the autumn weather
Compelled my imagination many days,
Many days and many hours:
Her hair over her arms and her arms full of flowers.
And I wonder how they should have been together!

I should have lost a gesture and a pose.
Sometimes these cogitations still amaze
The troubled midnight and the noon's repose.

POEMS

1920

GERONTION

Thou hast nor youth nor age
But as it were an after dinner sleep
Dreaming of both.

Here I am, an old man in a dry month,
Being read to by a boy, waiting for rain.
I was neither at the hot gates
Nor fought in the warm rain
Nor knee deep in the salt marsh, heaving a cutlass,
Bitten by flies, fought.
My house is a decayed house,
And the Jew squats on the window-sill, the owner,
Spawned in some estaminet of Antwerp,
Blistered in Brussels, patched and peeled in London.
The goat coughs at night in the field overhead;
Rocks, moss, stonecrop, iron, merds.
The woman keeps the kitchen, makes tea,
Sneezes at evening, poking the peevish gutter.
I an old man,
A dull head among windy spaces.

Signs are taken for wonders. 'We would see a sign!'
The word within a word, unable to speak a word,
Swaddled with darkness. In the juvescence of the year
Came Christ the tiger

In depraved May, dogwood and chestnut,
        flowering judas,
To be eaten, to be divided, to be drunk
Among whispers; by Mr Silvero
With caressing hands, at Limoges
Who walked all night in the next room;
By Hakagawa, bowing among the Titians;
By Madame de Tornquist, in the dark room
Shifting the candles; Fräulein von Kulp
Who turned in the hall, one hand on the door.
        Vacant shuttles
Weave the wind. I have no ghosts,
An old man in a draughty house
Under a windy knob.

After such knowledge, what forgiveness? Think now
History has many cunning passages, contrived
        corridors
And issues, deceives with whispering ambitions,
Guides us by vanities. Think now
She gives when our attention is distracted
And what she gives, gives with such supple confusions
That the giving famishes the craving. Gives too late
What's not believed in, or if still believed,
In memory only, reconsidered passion. Gives too soon
Into weak hands, what's thought can be dispensed with
Till the refusal propagates a fear. Think

Neither fear nor courage saves us. Unnatural vices
Are fathered by our heroism. Virtues
Are forced upon us by our impudent crimes.
These tears are shaken from the wrath-bearing tree.

The tiger springs in the new year. Us he devours.
        Think at last
We have not reached conclusion, when I
Stiffen in a rented house. Think at last
I have not made this show purposelessly
And it is not by any concitation
Of the backward devils.
I would meet you upon this honestly.
I that was near your heart was removed therefrom
To lose beauty in terror, terror in inquisition.
I have lost my passion: why should I need to keep it
Since what is kept must be adulterated?
I have lost my sight, smell, hearing, taste and touch:
How should I use them for your closer contact?

These with a thousand small deliberations
Protract the profit of their chilled delirium,
Excite the membrane, when the sense has cooled,
With pungent sauces, multiply variety
In a wilderness of mirrors. What will the spider do,
Suspend its operations, will the weevil
Delay? De Bailhache, Fresca, Mrs Cammel, whirled

Beyond the circuit of the shuddering Bear
In fractured atoms. Gull against the wind, in the
windy straits
Of Belle Isle, or running on the Horn.
White feathers in the snow, the Gulf claims,
And an old man driven by the Trades
To a sleepy corner.

Tenants of the house,
Thoughts of a dry brain in a dry season.

BURBANK WITH A BAEDEKER: BLEISTEIN WITH A CIGAR

Tra-la-la-la-la-la-laire—nil nisi divinum stabile est; caetera fumus—the gondola stopped, the old palace was there, how charming its grey and pink—goats and monkeys, with such hair too!—so the countess passed on until she came through the little park, where Niobe presented her with a cabinet, and so departed.

Burbank crossed a little bridge
  Descending at a small hotel;
Princess Volupine arrived,
  They were together, and he fell.

Defunctive music under sea
  Passed seaward with the passing bell
Slowly: the God Hercules
  Had left him, that had loved him well.

The horses, under the axletree
  Beat up the dawn from Istria
With even feet. Her shuttered barge
  Burned on the water all the day.

But this or such was Bleistein's way:
A saggy bending of the knees
And elbows, with the palms turned out,
Chicago Semite Viennese.

A lustreless protrusive eye
Stares from the protozoic slime
At a perspective of Canaletto.
The smoky candle end of time

Declines. On the Rialto once.
The rats are underneath the piles.
The Jew is underneath the lot.
Money in furs. The boatman smiles,

Princess Volupine extends
A meagre, blue-nailed, phthisic hand
To climb the waterstair. Lights, lights,
She entertains Sir Ferdinand

Klein. Who clipped the lion's wings
And flea'd his rump and pared his claws?
Thought Burbank, meditating on
Time's ruins, and the seven laws.

SWEENEY ERECT

And the trees about me,
Let them be dry and leafless; let the rocks
Groan with continual surges; and behind me
Make all a desolation. Look, look, wenches!

Paint me a cavernous waste shore
  Cast in the unstilled Cyclades,
Paint me the bold anfractuous rocks
  Faced by the snarled and yelping seas.

Display me Aeolus above
  Reviewing the insurgent gales
Which tangle Ariadne's hair
  And swell with haste the perjured sails.

Morning stirs the feet and hands
  (Nausicaa and Polypheme).
Gesture of orang-outang
  Rises from the sheets in steam.

This withered root of knots of hair
  Slitted below and gashed with eyes,
This oval O cropped out with teeth:
  The sickle motion from the thighs

Jackknifes upward at the knees
    Then straightens out from heel to hip
Pushing the framework of the bed
    And clawing at the pillow slip.

Sweeney addressed full length to shave
    Broadbottomed, pink from nape to base,
Knows the female temperament
    And wipes the suds around his face.

(The lengthened shadow of a man
    Is history, said Emerson
Who had not seen the silhouette
    Of Sweeney straddled in the sun.)

Tests the razor on his leg
    Waiting until the shriek subsides.
The epileptic on the bed
    Curves backward, clutching at her sides.

The ladies of the corridor
    Find themselves involved, disgraced,
Call witness to their principles
    And deprecate the lack of taste

Observing that hysteria
    Might easily be misunderstood;

Mrs Turner intimates
    It does the house no sort of good.

But Doris, towelled from the bath,
    Enters padding on broad feet,
Bringing sal volatile
    And a glass of brandy neat.

A COOKING EGG

En l'an trentiesme de mon aage
Que toutes mes hontes j'ay beues . . .

Pipit sate upright in her chair
  Some distance from where I was sitting;
Views of Oxford Colleges
  Lay on the table, with the knitting.

Daguerreotypes and silhouettes,
  Her grandfather and great great aunts,
Supported on the mantelpiece
  An *Invitation to the Dance.*

* * *

I shall not want Honour in Heaven
  For I shall meet Sir Philip Sidney
And have talk with Coriolanus
  And other heroes of that kidney.

I shall not want Capital in Heaven
  For I shall meet Sir Alfred Mond.
We two shall lie together, lapt
  In a five per cent Exchequer Bond.

I shall not want Society in Heaven,
  Lucretia Borgia shall be my Bride;
Her anecdotes will be more amusing
  Than Pipit's experience could provide.

I shall not want Pipit in Heaven:
  Madame Blavatsky will instruct me
In the Seven Sacred Trances;
  Piccarda de Donati will conduct me.

* * *

But where is the penny world I bought
  To eat with Pipit behind the screen?
The red-eyed scavengers are creeping
  From Kentish Town and Golder's Green;

Where are the eagles and the trumpets?

  Buried beneath some snow-deep Alps.
Over buttered scones and crumpets
  Weeping, weeping multitudes
Droop in a hundred A.B.C.'s.

LE DIRECTEUR

Malheur à la malheureuse Tamise
Qui coule si près du Spectateur.
Le directeur
Conservateur
Du Spectateur
Empeste la brise.
Les actionnaires
Réactionnaires
Du Spectateur
Conservateur
Bras dessus bras dessous
Font des tours
A pas de loup.
Dans un égout
Une petite fille
En guenilles
Camarde
Regarde
Le directeur
Du Spectateur
Conservateur
Et crève d'amour.

MÉLANGE ADULTÈRE DE TOUT

En Amérique, professeur;
En Angleterre, journaliste;
C'est à grands pas et en sueur
Que vous suivrez à peine ma piste.
En Yorkshire, conférencier;
A Londres, un peu banquier,
Vous me paierez bien la tête.
C'est à Paris que je me coiffe
Casque noir de jemenfoutiste.
En Allemagne, philosophe
Surexcité par Emporheben
Au grand air de Bergsteigleben;
J'erre toujours de-ci de-là
A divers coups de tra là là
De Damas jusqu'à Omaha.
Je célébrai mon jour de fête
Dans une oasis d'Afrique
Vêtu d'une peau de girafe.

On montrera mon cénotaphe
Aux côtes brûlantes de Mozambique.

LUNE DE MIEL

Ils ont vu les Pay-Bas, ils rentrent à Terre Haute;
Mais une nuit d'été, les voici à Ravenne,
A l'aise entre deux draps, chez deux centaines
    de punaises;
La sueur aestivale, et une forte odeur de chienne.
Ils restent sur le dos écartent les genoux
De quatre jambes molles tout gonflées de morsures.
On relève le drap pour mieux égratigner.
Moins d'une lieue d'ici est Saint Apollinaire
En Classe, basilique connue des amateurs
De chapitaux d'acanthe que tournoie le vent.

Ils vont prendre le train de huit heures
Prolonger leurs misères de Padoue à Milan
Où se trouve la Cène, et un restaurant pas cher.
Lui pense aux pourboires, et rédige son bilan.
Ils auront vu la Suisse et traversé la France.
Et Saint Apollinaire, raide et ascétique,
Vieille usine désaffectée de Dieu, tient encore
Dans ses pierres écroulantes la forme précise
    de Byzance.

THE HIPPOPOTAMUS

And when this epistle is read among you, cause that it be read also in the church of the Laodiceans.

The broad-backed hippopotamus
Rests on his belly in the mud;
Although he seems so firm to us
He is merely flesh and blood.

Flesh and blood is weak and frail,
Susceptible to nervous shock;
While the True Church can never fail
For it is based upon a rock.

The hippo's feeble steps may err
In compassing material ends,
While the True Church need never stir
To gather in its dividends.

The 'potamus can never reach
The mango on the mango-tree;
But fruits of pomegranate and peach
Refresh the Church from over sea.

At mating time the hippo's voice
Betrays inflexions hoarse and odd,

But every week we hear rejoice
The Church, at being one with God.

The hippopotamus's day
Is passed in sleep; at night he hunts;
God works in a mysterious way—
The Church can sleep and feed at once.

I saw the 'potamus take wing
Ascending from the damp savannas,
And quiring angels round him sing
The praise of God, in loud hosannas.

Blood of the Lamb shall wash him clean
And him shall heavenly arms enfold,
Among the saints he shall be seen
Performing on a harp of gold.

He shall be washed as white as snow,
By all the martyr'd virgins kist,
While the True Church remains below
Wrapt in the old miasmal mist.

DANS LE RESTAURANT

Le garçon délabré qui n'a rien à faire
Que de se gratter les doigts et se pencher sur mon
    épaule:
  'Dans mon pays il fera temps pluvieux,
  Du vent, du grand soleil, et de la pluie;
  C'est ce qu'on appelle le jour de lessive des gueux.'
(Bavard, baveux, à la croupe arrondie,
Je te prie, au moins, ne bave pas dans la soupe).
  'Les saules trempés, et des bourgeons sur les
    ronces—
  C'est là, dans une averse, qu'on s'abrite.
J'avais sept ans, elle était plus petite.
  Ellé était toute mouillée, je lui ai donné des
    primevères.'
Les taches de son gilet montent au chiffre de trente-
    huit.
  'Je la chatouillais, pour la faire rire.
  J'éprouvais un instant de puissance et de délire.'

  Mais alors, vieux lubrique, à cet âge...
'Monsieur, le fait est dur.
  Il est venu, nous peloter, un gros chien;
  Moi j'avais peur, je l'ai quittée à mi-chemin.
  C'est dommage.'
    Mais alors, tu as ton vautour!

Va t'en te décrotter les rides du visage;
Tiens, ma fourchette, décrasse-toi le crâne.
De quel droit payes-tu des expériences comme moi?
Tiens, voilà dix sous, pour la salle-de-bains.

Phlébas, le Phénicien, pendant quinze jours noyé,
Oubliait les cris des mouettes et la houle de
    Cornouaille,
Et les profits et les pertes, et la cargaison d'étain:
Un courant de sous-mer l'emporta très loin,
Le repassant aux étapes de sa vie antérieure.
Figurez-vous donc, c'était un sort pénible;
Cependant, ce fut jadis un bel homme, de haute taille.

WHISPERS OF IMMORTALITY

Webster was much possessed by death
And saw the skull beneath the skin;
And breastless creatures under ground
Leaned backward with a lipless grin.

Daffodil bulbs instead of balls
Stared from the sockets of the eyes!
He knew that thought clings round dead limbs
Tightening its lusts and luxuries.

Donne, I suppose, was such another
Who found no substitute for sense,
To seize and clutch and penetrate;
Expert beyond experience,

He knew the anguish of the marrow
The ague of the skeleton;
No contact possible to flesh
Allayed the fever of the bone.

* * *

Grishkin is nice: her Russian eye
Is underlined for emphasis;
Uncorseted, her friendly bust
Gives promise of pneumatic bliss.

The couched Brazilian jaguar
Compels the scampering marmoset
With subtle effluence of cat;
Grishkin has a maisonnette;

The sleek Brazilian jaguar
Does not in its arboreal gloom
Distil so rank a feline smell
As Grishkin in a drawing-room.

And even the Abstract Entities
Circumambulate her charm;
But our lot crawls between dry ribs
To keep our metaphysics warm.

MR ELIOT'S SUNDAY MORNING SERVICE

Look, look, master, here comes two religious caterpillars.

THE JEW OF MALTA

Polyphiloprogenitive
The sapient sutlers of the Lord
Drift across the window-panes.
In the beginning was the Word.

In the beginning was the Word.
Superfetation of *τὸ ἕν*,
And at the mensual turn of time
Produced enervate Origen.

A painter of the Umbrian school
Designed upon a gesso ground
The nimbus of the Baptized God.
The wilderness is cracked and browned.

But through the water pale and thin
Still shine the unoffending feet
And there above the painter set
The Father and the Paraclete.

* * *

The sable presbyters approach
The avenue of penitence;
The young are red and pustular
Clutching piaculative pence.

Under the penitential gates
Sustained by staring Seraphim
Where the souls of the devout
Burn invisible and dim.

Along the garden-wall the bees
With hairy bellies pass between
The staminate and pistillate,
Blest office of the epicene.

Sweeney shifts from ham to ham
Stirring the water in his bath.
The masters of the subtle schools
Are controversial, polymath.

SWEENEY AMONG THE NIGHTINGALES

ὤμοι, πέπληγμαι καιρίαν πληγὴν ἔσω.

Apeneck Sweeney spreads his knees
Letting his arms hang down to laugh,
The zebra stripes along his jaw
Swelling to maculate giraffe.

The circles of the stormy moon
Slide westward toward the River Plate,
Death and the Raven drift above
And Sweeney guards the hornèd gate.

Gloomy Orion and the Dog
Are veiled; and hushed the shrunken seas;
The person in the Spanish cape
Tries to sit on Sweeney's knees

Slips and pulls the table cloth
Overturns a coffee-cup,
Reorganised upon the floor
She yawns and draws a stocking up;

The silent man in mocha brown
Sprawls at the window-sill and gapes;

The waiter brings in oranges
Bananas figs and hothouse grapes;

The silent vertebrate in brown
Contracts and concentrates, withdraws;
Rachel *née* Rabinovitch
Tears at the grapes with murderous paws;

She and the lady in the cape
Are suspect, thought to be in league;
Therefore the man with heavy eyes
Declines the gambit, shows fatigue,

Leaves the room and reappears
Outside the window, leaning in,
Branches of wistaria
Circumscribe a golden grin;

The host with someone indistinct
Converses at the door apart,
The nightingales are singing near
The Convent of the Sacred Heart,

And sang within the bloody wood
When Agamemnon cried aloud
And let their liquid siftings fall
To stain the stiff dishonoured shroud.

THE WASTE LAND

'Nam Sibyllam quidem Cumis ego ipse oculis meis vidi in ampulla pendere, et cum illi pueri dicerent: *Σίβυλλα τί θέλεις*; respondebat illa: *ἀποθανεῖν θέλω.*'

For Ezra Pound
il miglior fabbro.

I. THE BURIAL OF THE DEAD

April is the cruellest month, breeding
Lilacs out of the dead land, mixing
Memory and desire, stirring
Dull roots with spring rain.
Winter kept us warm, covering
Earth in forgetful snow, feeding
A little life with dried tubers.
Summer surprised us, coming over the Starnbergersee
With a shower of rain; we stopped in the colonnade,
And went on in sunlight, into the Hofgarten,
And drank coffee, and talked for an hour.
Bin gar keine Russin, stamm' aus Litauen, echt
deutsch.
And when we were children, staying at the arch-duke's,
My cousin's, he took me out on a sled,
And I was frightened. He said, Marie,
Marie, hold on tight. And down we went.
In the mountains, there you feel free.
I read, much of the night, and go south in the winter.

What are the roots that clutch, what branches grow
Out of this stony rubbish? Son of man,
You cannot say, or guess, for you know only
A heap of broken images, where the sun beats,
And the dead tree gives no shelter, the cricket no relief,

And the dry stone no sound of water. Only
There is shadow under this red rock,
(Come in under the shadow of this red rock),
And I will show you something different from either
Your shadow at morning striding behind you
Or your shadow at evening rising to meet you;
I will show you fear in a handful of dust.

Frisch weht der Wind
Der Heimat zu
Mein Irisch Kind,
Wo weilest du?

'You gave me Hyacinths first a year ago;
'They called me the hyacinth girl.'
—Yet when we came back, late, from the hyacinth garden,
Your arms full, and your hair wet, I could not
Speak, and my eyes failed, I was neither
Living nor dead, and I knew nothing,
Looking into the heart of light, the silence.
Oed' und leer das Meer.

Madame Sosostris, famous clairvoyante,
Had a bad cold, nevertheless
Is known to be the wisest woman in Europe,
With a wicked pack of cards. Here, said she,
Is your card, the drowned Phoenician Sailor,
(Those are pearls that were his eyes. Look!)

Here is Belladonna, the Lady of the Rocks,
The lady of situations.
Here is the man with three staves, and here the Wheel,
And here is the one-eyed merchant, and this card,
Which is blank, is something he carries on his back,
Which I am forbidden to see. I do not find
The Hanged Man. Fear death by water.
I see crowds of people, walking round in a ring.
Thank you. If you see dear Mrs Equitone,
Tell her I bring the horoscope myself:
One must be so careful these days.

Unreal City,
Under the brown fog of a winter dawn,
A crowd flowed over London Bridge, so many,
I had not thought death had undone so many.
Sighs, short and infrequent, were exhaled,
And each man fixed his eyes before his feet.
Flowed up the hill and down King William Street,
To where Saint Mary Woolnoth kept the hours
With a dead sound on the final stroke of nine.
There I saw one I knew, and stopped him, crying:
'Stetson!
'You who were with me in the ships at Mylae!
'That corpse you planted last year in your garden,
'Has it begun to sprout? Will it bloom this year?
'Or has the sudden frost disturbed its bed?

'O keep the Dog far hence, that's friend to men,
'Or with his nails he'll dig it up again!
'You! hypocrite lecteur!—mon semblable,—mon frère!'

II. A GAME OF CHESS

The Chair she sat in, like a burnished throne,
Glowed on the marble, where the glass
Held up by standards wrought with fruited vines
From which a golden Cupidon peeped out
(Another hid his eyes behind his wing)
Doubled the flames of sevenbranched candelabra
Reflecting light upon the table as
The glitter of her jewels rose to meet it,
From satin cases poured in rich profusion.
In vials of ivory and coloured glass
Unstoppered, lurked her strange synthetic perfumes,
Unguent, powdered, or liquid—troubled, confused
And drowned the sense in odours; stirred by the air
That freshened from the window, these ascended
In fattening the prolonged candle-flames,
Flung their smoke into the laquearia,
Stirring the pattern on the coffered ceiling.
Huge sea-wood fed with copper
Burned green and orange, framed by the coloured
    stone,
In which sad light a carvèd dolphin swam.
Above the antique mantel was displayed
As though a window gave upon the sylvan scene
The change of Philomel, by the barbarous king
So rudely forced; yet there the nightingale

Filled all the desert with inviolable voice
And still she cried, and still the world pursues,
'Jug Jug' to dirty ears.
And other withered stumps of time
Were told upon the walls; staring forms
Leaned out, leaning, hushing the room enclosed.
Footsteps shuffled on the stair.
Under the firelight, under the brush, her hair
Spread out in fiery points
Glowed into words, then would be savagely still.

'My nerves are bad to-night. Yes, bad. Stay with me.
Speak to me. Why do you never speak? Speak.
What are you thinking of? What thinking?
What?
I never know what you are thinking. Think.'

I think we are in rats' alley
Where the dead men lost their bones.

'What is that noise?'
The wind under the door.
'What is that noise now? What is the wind doing?'
Nothing again nothing.
'Do
You know nothing? Do you see nothing? Do you
remember
'Nothing?'

I remember
Those are pearls that were his eyes.
'Are you alive, or not? Is there nothing in your head?'
But

O O O O that Shakespeherian Rag—
It's so elegant
So intelligent
'What shall I do now? What shall I do?
I shall rush out as I am, and walk the street
With my hair down, so. What shall we do tomorrow?
What shall we ever do?'
The hot water at ten.
And if it rains, a closed car at four.
And we shall play a game of chess,
Pressing lidless eyes and waiting for a knock upon
the door.

When Lil's husband got demobbed, I said—
I didn't mince my words, I said to her myself,
HURRY UP PLEASE ITS TIME
Now Albert's coming back, make yourself a bit smart.
He'll want to know what you done with that money
he gave you
To get yourself some teeth. He did, I was there.
You have them all out, Lil, and get a nice set,
He said, I swear, I can't bear to look at you.
And no more can't I, I said, and think of poor Albert,

He's been in the army four years, he wants a good time,
And if you don't give it him, there's others will, I said.
Oh is there, she said. Something o' that, I said.
Then I'll know who to thank, she said, and give me a straight look.
HURRY UP PLEASE ITS TIME
If you don't like it you can get on with it, I said.
Others can pick and choose if you can't.
But if Albert makes off, it won't be for lack of telling.
You ought to be ashamed, I said, to look so antique.
(And her only thirty-one.)
I can't help it, she said, pulling a long face,
It's them pills I took, to bring it off, she said.
(She's had five already, and nearly died of young George.)
The chemist said it would be all right, but I've never been the same.
You *are* a proper fool, I said.
Well, if Albert won't leave you alone, there it is, I said,
What you get married for if you don't want children?
HURRY UP PLEASE ITS TIME
Well, that Sunday Albert was home, they had a hot gammon,
And they asked me in to dinner, to get the beauty of it hot—
HURRY UP PLEASE ITS TIME
HURRY UP PLEASE ITS TIME

Goonight Bill. Goonight Lou. Goonight May. Goonight.
Ta ta. Goonight. Goonight.
Good night, ladies, good night, sweet ladies, good night, good night.

III. THE FIRE SERMON

The river's tent is broken; the last fingers of leaf
Clutch and sink into the wet bank. The wind
Crosses the brown land, unheard. The nymphs
are departed.
Sweet Thames, run softly, till I end my song.
The river bears no empty bottles, sandwich papers,
Silk handkerchiefs, cardboard boxes, cigarette ends
Or other testimony of summer nights. The nymphs
are departed.
And their friends, the loitering heirs of City
directors;
Departed, have left no addresses.
By the waters of Leman I sat down and wept...
Sweet Thames, run softly till I end my song,
Sweet Thames, run softly, for I speak not loud
or long.
But at my back in a cold blast I hear
The rattle of the bones, and chuckle spread from
ear to ear.

A rat crept softly through the vegetation
Dragging its slimy belly on the bank
While I was fishing in the dull canal
On a winter evening round behind the gashouse
Musing upon the king my brother's wreck

And on the king my father's death before him.
White bodies naked on the low damp ground
And bones cast in a little low dry garret,
Rattled by the rat's foot only, year to year.
But at my back from time to time I hear
The sound of horns and motors, which
    shall bring
Sweeney to Mrs Porter in the spring.
O the moon shone bright on Mrs Porter
And on her daughter
They wash their feet in soda water
Et O ces voix d'enfants, chantant dans la coupole!

Twit twit twit
Jug jug jug jug jug jug
So rudely forc'd.
Tereu

  Unreal City
Under the brown fog of a winter noon
Mr Eugenides, the Smyrna merchant
Unshaven, with a pocket full of currants
C.i.f. London: documents at sight,
Asked me in demotic French
To luncheon at the Cannon Street Hotel
Followed by a weekend at the Metropole.

At the violet hour, when the eyes and back
Turn upward from the desk, when the human engine waits
Like a taxi throbbing waiting,
I Tiresias, though blind, throbbing between two lives,
Old man with wrinkled female breasts, can see
At the violet hour, the evening hour that strives
Homeward, and brings the sailor home from sea,
The typist home at teatime, clears her breakfast, lights
Her stove, and lays out food in tins.
Out of the window perilously spread
Her drying combinations touched by the sun's last rays,
On the divan are piled (at night her bed)
Stockings, slippers, camisoles, and stays.
I Tiresias, old man with wrinkled dugs
Perceived the scene, and foretold the rest—
I too awaited the expected guest.
He, the young man carbuncular, arrives,
A small house agent's clerk, with one bold stare,
One of the low on whom assurance sits
As a silk hat on a Bradford millionaire.
The time is now propitious, as he guesses,
The meal is ended, she is bored and tired,
Endeavours to engage her in caresses
Which still are unreproved, if undesired.
Flushed and decided, he assaults at once;
Exploring hands encounter no defence;

His vanity requires no response,
And makes a welcome of indifference.
(And I Tiresias have foresuffered all
Enacted on this same divan or bed;
I who have sat by Thebes below the wall
And walked among the lowest of the dead.)
Bestows one final patronising kiss,
And gropes his way, finding the stairs unlit...

She turns and looks a moment in the glass,
Hardly aware of her departed lover;
Her brain allows one half-formed thought to pass:
'Well now that's done: and I'm glad it's over.'
When lovely woman stoops to folly and
Paces about her room again, alone,
She smooths her hair with automatic hand,
And puts a record on the gramophone.

'This music crept by me upon the waters'
And along the Strand, up Queen Victoria Street.
O City city, I can sometimes hear
Beside a public bar in Lower Thames Street,
The pleasant whining of a mandoline
And a clatter and a chatter from within
Where fishmen lounge at noon: where the walls
Of Magnus Martyr hold
Inexplicable splendour of Ionian white and gold.

The river sweats
Oil and tar
The barges drift
With the turning tide
Red sails
Wide
To leeward, swing on the heavy spar.
The barges wash
Drifting logs
Down Greenwich reach
Past the Isle of Dogs.
                Weialala leia
                Wallala leialala

Elizabeth and Leicester
Beating oars
The stern was formed
A gilded shell
Red and gold
The brisk swell
Rippled both shores
Southwest wind
Carried down stream
The peal of bells
White towers
                Weialala leia
                Wallala leialala

'Trams and dusty trees.
Highbury bore me. Richmond and Kew
Undid me. By Richmond I raised my knees
Supine on the floor of a narrow canoe.'

'My feet are at Moorgate, and my heart
Under my feet. After the event
He wept. He promised "a new start."
I made no comment. What should I resent?'

'On Margate Sands.
I can connect
Nothing with nothing.
The broken fingernails of dirty hands.
My people humble people who expect
Nothing.'
                    la la

To Carthage then I came

Burning burning burning burning
O Lord Thou pluckest me out
O Lord Thou pluckest

burning

IV. DEATH BY WATER

Phlebas the Phoenician, a fortnight dead,
Forgot the cry of gulls, and the deep sea swell
And the profit and loss.
                                        A current under sea
Picked his bones in whispers. As he rose and fell
He passed the stages of his age and youth
Entering the whirlpool.
                                        Gentile or Jew
O you who turn the wheel and look to windward,
Consider Phlebas, who was once handsome and
      tall as you.

V. WHAT THE THUNDER SAID

After the torchlight red on sweaty faces
After the frosty silence in the gardens
After the agony in stony places
The shouting and the crying
Prison and palace and reverberation
Of thunder of spring over distant mountains
He who was living is now dead
We who were living are now dying
With a little patience

Here is no water but only rock
Rock and no water and the sandy road
The road winding above among the mountains
Which are mountains of rock without water
If there were water we should stop and drink
Amongst the rock one cannot stop or think
Sweat is dry and feet are in the sand
If there were only water amongst the rock
Dead mountain mouth of carious teeth that cannot spit
Here one can neither stand nor lie nor sit
There is not even silence in the mountains
But dry sterile thunder without rain
There is not even solitude in the mountains
But red sullen faces sneer and snarl

From doors of mudcracked houses
                    If there were water
   And no rock
   If there were rock
   And also water
   And water
   A spring
   A pool among the rock
   If there were the sound of water only
   Not the cicada
   And dry grass singing
   But sound of water over a rock
   Where the hermit-thrush sings in the pine trees
   Drip drop drip drop drop drop drop
   But there is no water

   Who is the third who walks always beside you?
When I count, there are only you and I together
But when I look ahead up the white road
There is always another one walking beside you
Gliding wrapt in a brown mantle, hooded
I do not know whether a man or a woman
—But who is that on the other side of you?

   What is that sound high in the air
Murmur of maternal lamentation
Who are those hooded hordes swarming

Over endless plains, stumbling in cracked earth
Ringed by the flat horizon only
What is the city over the mountains
Cracks and reforms and bursts in the violet air
Falling towers
Jerusalem Athens Alexandria
Vienna London
Unreal

A woman drew her long black hair out tight
And fiddled whisper music on those strings
And bats with baby faces in the violet light
Whistled, and beat their wings
And crawled head downward down a blackened wall
And upside down in air were towers
Tolling reminiscent bells, that kept the hours
And voices singing out of empty cisterns and
exhausted wells.

In this decayed hole among the mountains
In the faint moonlight, the grass is singing
Over the tumbled graves, about the chapel
There is the empty chapel, only the wind's home.
It has no windows, and the door swings,
Dry bones can harm no one.
Only a cock stood on the rooftree
Co co rico co co rico

In a flash of lightning. Then a damp gust
Bringing rain

Ganga was sunken, and the limp leaves
Waited for rain, while the black clouds
Gathered far distant, over Himavant.
The jungle crouched, humped in silence.
Then spoke the thunder
DA
Datta: what have we given?
My friend, blood shaking my heart
The awful daring of a moment's surrender
Which an age of prudence can never retract
By this, and this only, we have existed
Which is not to be found in our obituaries
Or in memories draped by the beneficent spider
Or under seals broken by the lean solicitor
In our empty rooms
DA
Dayadhvam: I have heard the key
Turn in the door once and turn once only
We think of the key, each in his prison
Thinking of the key, each confirms a prison
Only at nightfall, aethereal rumours
Revive for a moment a broken Coriolanus
DA
Damyata: The boat responded

Gaily, to the hand expert with sail and oar
The sea was calm, your heart would have
    responded
Gaily, when invited, beating obedient
To controlling hands

                                        I sat upon the shore
Fishing, with the arid plain behind me
Shall I at least set my lands in order?
London Bridge is falling down falling down falling
    down
Poi s'ascose nel foco che gli affina
Quando fiam uti chelidon—O swallow swallow
Le Prince d'Aquitaine à la tour abolie
These fragments I have shored against my ruins
Why then Ile fit you. Hieronymo's mad againe.
Datta. Dayadhvam. Damyata.
                    Shantih shantih shantih

NOTES ON THE WASTE LAND

Not only the title, but the plan and a good deal of the incidental symbolism of the poem were suggested by Miss Jessie L. Weston's book on the Grail legend: *From Ritual to Romance* (Cambridge). Indeed, so deeply am I indebted, Miss Weston's book will elucidate the difficulties of the poem much better than my notes can do; and I recommend it (apart from the great interest of the book itself) to any who think such elucidation of the poem worth the trouble. To another work of anthropology I am indebted in general, one which has influenced our generation profoundly; I mean *The Golden Bough*; I have used especially the two volumes *Adonis, Attis, Osiris.* Anyone who is acquainted with these works will immediately recognise in the poem certain references to vegetation ceremonies.

I. THE BURIAL OF THE DEAD

Line 20. Cf. Ezekiel II, i.

23. Cf. Ecclesiastes XII, v.

31. V. Tristan und Isolde, I, verses 5–8

42. Id. III, verse 24.

46. I am not familiar with the exact constitution of the Tarot pack of cards, from which I have obviously departed to suit my own convenience. The Hanged Man, a member of the traditional pack, fits my purpose

in two ways: because he is associated in my mind with the Hanged God of Frazer, and because I associate him with the hooded figure in the passage of the disciples to Emmaus in Part V. The Phoenician Sailor and the Merchant appear later; also the 'crowds of people', and Death by Water is executed in Part IV. The Man with Three Staves (an authentic member of the Tarot pack) I associate, quite arbitrarily, with the Fisher King himself.

60. Cf. Baudelaire:

'Fourmillante cité, cité pleine de rêves,
'Ou le spectre en plein jour raccroche le passant.'

63. Cf. Inferno III, 55–57:

si lunga tratta
di gente, ch'io non averei creduto
che morte tanta n'avesse disfatta.

64. Cf. Inferno IV, 25–27:

Quivi, secondo che per ascoltare,
non avea piante mai che di sospiri
che l'aura eterna facevan tremare.

68. A phenomenon which I have often noticed.

74. Cf. the Dirge in Webster's *White Devil.*

76. V. Baudelaire, Preface to *Fleurs du Mal.*

II. A GAME OF CHESS

77. Cf. *Antony and Cleopatra,* II, ii, l. 190.

92. Laquearia. V. *Aeneid*, I, 726:

dependent lychni laquearibus aureis
incensi, et noctem flammis funalia vincunt.

98. Sylvan scene. V. Milton, *Paradise Lost*, IV, 140.

99. V. Ovid, *Metamorphoses*, VI, Philomela.

100. Cf. Part III, l. 204.

115. Cf. Part III, l. 195.

118. Cf. Webster: 'Is the wind in that door still?'

126. Cf. Part I, l. 37, 48.

138. Cf. the game of chess in Middleton's *Women beware Women*.

III. THE FIRE SERMON

176. V. Spenser, *Prothalamion*.

192. Cf. *The Tempest*, I, ii.

196. Cf. Marvell, *To His Coy Mistress*.

197. Cf. Day, *Parliament of Bees:*

'When of the sudden, listening, you shall hear,
'A noise of horns and hunting, which shall bring
'Actaeon to Diana in the spring,
'Where all shall see her naked skin . . .'

199. I do not know the origin of the ballad from which these lines are taken: it was reported to me from Sydney, Australia.

202. V. Verlaine, *Parsifal*.

210. The currants were quoted at a price 'cost insurance and freight to London'; and the Bill of Lading,

etc., were to be handed to the buyer upon payment of the sight draft.

218. Tiresias, although a mere spectator and not indeed a 'character', is yet the most important personage in the poem, uniting all the rest. Just as the one-eyed merchant seller of currants, melts into the Phoenician Sailor, and the latter is not wholly distinct from Ferdinand Prince of Naples, so all the women are one woman, and the two sexes meet in Tiresias. What Tiresias *sees*, in fact, is the substance of the poem. The whole passage from Ovid is of great anthropological interest:

. . . Cum Iunone iocos et 'maior vestra profecto est
Quam quae contingit maribus', dixisse, 'voluptas.'
Illa negat; placuit quae sit sententia docti
Quaerere Tiresiae: venus huic erat utraque nota.
Nam duo magnorum viridi coeuntia silva
Corpora serpentum baculi violaverat ictu
Deque viro factus, mirabile, femina septem
Egerat autumnos; octavo rursus eosdem
Vidit et 'est vestrae si tanta potentia plagae',
Dixit 'ut auctoris sortem in contraria mutet,
Nunc quoque vos feriam!' percussis anguibus isdem
Forma prior rediit genetivaque venit imago.
Arbiter hic igitur sumptus de lite iocosa
Dicta Iovis firmat; gravius Saturnia iusto
Nec pro materia fertur doluisse suique
Iudicis aeterna damnavit lumina nocte,

At pater omnipotens (neque enim licet inrita cuiquam
Facta dei fecisse deo) pro lumine adempto
Scire futura dedit poenamque levavit honore.

221. This may not appear as exact as Sappho's lines, but I had in mind the 'longshore' or 'dory' fisherman, who returns at nightfall.

253. V. Goldsmith, the song in *The Vicar of Wakefield.*

257. V. *The Tempest,* as above.

264. The interior of St Magnus Martyr is to my mind one of the finest among Wren's interiors. See *The Proposed Demolition of Nineteen City Churches* (P. S. King & Son, Ltd).

266. The Song of the (three) Thames-daughters begins here. From line 292 to 306 inclusive they speak in turn. V. *Götterdämmerung*, III, i: the Rhine-daughters.

279. V. Froude, *Elizabeth,* Vol. I, ch. iv, letter of De Quadra to Philip of Spain:

'In the afternoon we were in a barge, watching the games on the river. (The Queen) was alone with Lord Robert and myself on the poop, when they began to talk nonsense, and went so far that Lord Robert at last said, as I was on the spot there was no reason why they should not be married if the queen pleased.'

293. Cf. *Purgatorio,* V. 133:

> 'Ricorditi di me, che son la Pia;
> 'Siena mi fe', disfecemi Maremma.'

307. V. St Augustine's *Confessions:* 'to Carthage then

I came, where a cauldron of unholy loves sang all about mine ears.'

308. The complete text of the Buddha's Fire Sermon (which corresponds in importance to the Sermon on the Mount) from which these words are taken, will be found translated in the late Henry Clarke Warren's *Buddhism in Translation* (Harvard Oriental Series). Mr Warren was one of the great pioneers of Buddhist studies in the Occident.

309. From St Augustine's *Confessions* again. The collocation of these two representatives of eastern and western asceticism, as the culmination of this part of the poem, is not an accident.

V. WHAT THE THUNDER SAID

In the first part of Part V three themes are employed: the journey to Emmaus, the approach to the Chapel Perilous (see Miss Weston's book) and the present decay of eastern Europe.

357. This is *Turdus aonalaschkae pallasii*, the hermit-thrush which I have heard in Quebec Province. Chapman says (*Handbook of Birds of Eastern North America*) 'it is most at home in secluded woodland and thickety retreats.... Its notes are not remarkable for variety or volume, but in purity and sweetness of tone and exquisite modulation they are unequalled.' Its 'water-dripping song' is justly celebrated.

360. The following lines were stimulated by the account of one of the Antarctic expeditions (I forget which, but I think one of Shackleton's): it was related that the party of explorers, at the extremity of their strength, had the constant delusion that there was *one more member* than could actually be counted.

366–76. Cf. Hermann Hesse, *Blick ins Chaos:* 'Schon ist halb Europa, schon ist zumindest der halbe Osten Europas auf dem Wege zum Chaos, fährt betrunken im heiligen Wahn am Abgrund entlang und singt dazu, singt betrunken und hymnisch wie Dmitri Karamasoff sang. Ueber diese Lieder lacht der Bürger beleidigt, der Heilige und Seher hört sie mit Tränen.'

401. 'Datta, dayadhvam, damyata' (Give, sympathise, control). The fable of the meaning of the Thunder is found in the *Brihadaranyaka—Upanishad*, 5, 1. A translation is found in Deussen's *Sechzig Upanishads des Veda*, p. 489.

407. Cf. Webster, *The White Devil*, V, vi:

'... they'll remarry
Ere the worm pierce your winding-sheet, ere the spider
Make a thin curtain for your epitaphs.'

411. Cf. *Inferno*, XXXIII, 46:

'ed io senti chiavar l'uscio di sotto
all' orribile torre.'

Also F. H. Bradley, *Appearance and Reality*, p. 306. 'My external sensations are no less private to my self than are my thoughts or my feelings. In either case my experience falls within my own circle, a circle closed on the outside; and, with all its elements alike, every sphere is opaque to the others which surround it.... In brief, regarded as an existence which appears in a soul, the whole world for each is peculiar and private to that soul.'

424. V. Weston: *From Ritual to Romance*; chapter on the Fisher King.

427. V. *Purgatorio*, XXVI, 148.

'"Ara vos prec per aquella valor
"que vos condus al som de l'escalina,
"sovenha vos a temps de ma dolor."
Poi s'ascose nel foco che li affina.'

428. V. *Pervigilium Veneris*. Cf. Philomela in Parts II and III.

429. V. Gerard de Nerval, Sonnet *El Desdichado*.

431. V. Kyd's *Spanish Tragedy*.

433. Shantih. Repeated as here, a formal ending to an Upanishad. 'The Peace which passeth understanding' is our equivalent to this word.

ESSAYS

REFLECTIONS ON *VERS LIBRE*

> *Ceux qui possèdent* leur *vers libre y tiennent:*
> *on n'abandonne que* le *vers libre.*
> DUHAMEL ET VILDRAC.

A lady, renowned in her small circle for the accuracy of her stop-press information of literature, complains to me of a growing pococurantism. 'Since the Russians came in I can read nothing else. I have finished Dostoevski, and I do not know what to do.' I suggested that the great Russian was an admirer of Dickens, and that she also might find that author readable. 'But Dickens is a sentimentalist; Dostoevski is a realist.' I reflected on the amours of Sonia and Rashkolnikov, but forbore to press the point, and I proposed *It Is Never too Late to Mend.* 'But one cannot read the Victorians at all!' While I was extracting the virtues of the proposition that Dostoevski is a Christian, while Charles Reade is merely pious, she added that she could no longer read any verse but *vers libre.*

It is assumed that *vers libre* exists. It is assumed that *vers libre* is a school; that it consists of certain theories; that its group or groups of theorists will either revolutionize or demoralize poetry if their attack upon the iambic pentameter meets with any success. *Vers libre* does not exist, and it is time that this preposterous fiction followed the *élan vital* and the eighty thousand Russians into oblivion.

When a theory of art passes it is usually found that a groat's worth of art has been bought with a million of advertisement. The theory which sold the wares may be quite false, or it may be confused and incapable of elucidation, or it may never have existed. A mythical revolution will have taken place and produced a few works of art which perhaps would be even better if still less of the revolutionary theories clung to them. In modern society such revolutions are almost inevitable. An artist happens upon a method, perhaps quite unreflectingly, which is new in the sense that it is essentially different from that of the second-rate people about him, and different in everything but essentials from that of any of his great predecessors. The novelty meets with neglect; neglect provokes attack; and attack demands a theory. In an ideal state of society one might imagine the good New growing naturally out of the good Old, without the need for polemic and theory; this would be a society with a living tradition. In a sluggish society, as actual societies are, tradition is ever lapsing into superstition, and the violent stimulus of novelty is required. This is bad for the artist and his school, who may become circumscribed by their theory and narrowed by their polemic; but the artist can always console himself for his errors in his old age by considering that if he had not fought nothing would have been accomplished.

Vers libre has not even the excuse of a polemic; it is a battle-cry of freedom, and there is no freedom in art. And as the so-called *vers libre* which is good is anything but 'free', it can better be defended under some other label. Particular types of *vers libre* may be supported on the choice of content, or on the method of handling the content. I am aware that many writers of *vers libre* have introduced such innovations, and that the novelty of their choice and manipulation of material is confused – if not in their own minds, in the minds of many of their readers – with the novelty of the form. But I am not here concerned with imagism, which is a theory about the use of material; I am only concerned with the theory of the verse-form in which imagism is cast. If *vers libre* is a genuine verse-form it will have a positive definition. And I can define it only in negatives: (1) absence of pattern, (2) absence of rhyme, (3) absence of metre.

The third of these qualities is easily disposed of. What sort of a line that would be which would not scan at all I cannot say. Even in the popular American magazines, whose verse columns are now largely given over to *vers libre*, the lines are usually explicable in terms of prosody. Any line can be divided into feet and accents. The simpler metres are a repetition of one combination, perhaps a long and a short, or a short and a long syllable, five times repeated. There is, however, no reason why, within the single line, there should be any repetition; why there should not be lines (as there are) divisible only into feet of different types. How can the grammatical exercise of scansion make a line of this sort more intelligible? Only by isolating elements which occur in other lines, and the sole purpose of doing this is the production of a similar effect elsewhere. But repetition of effect is a question of pattern.

Scansion tells us very little. It is probable that there is not much to be gained by an elaborate system of prosody, but the erudite complexities of Swinburnian metre. With Swinburne, once the trick is perceived and the scholarship appreciated, the effect is somewhat diminished. When the unexpectedness, due to the unfamiliarity of the metres to English ears, wears off and is understood, one ceases to look for what one does not find in Swinburne; the inexplicable line with the music which can never be recaptured in other words. Swinburne mastered his technique, which is a great deal, but he did not master it to the extent of being able to take liberties with it, which is everything. If anything promising for English poetry is hidden in the metres of Swinburne, it probably lies far beyond the point to which Swinburne has developed them. But the most interesting verse which has yet been written in our language has been done either by taking a very simple form, like the iambic pentameter, and constantly withdrawing from it, or taking no form at all, and constantly approximating to a very simple one. It is this contrast between fixity and flux, this unperceived evasion of monotony, which is the very life of verse.

I have in mind two passages of contemporary verse which would be called *vers libre*. Both of them I quote because of their beauty:

> *Once, in finesse of fiddles found I ecstasy,*
> *In the flash of gold heels on the hard pavement.*
> *Now see I*
> *That warmth's the very stuff of poesy.*
> *Oh, God, make small*
> *The old star-eaten blanket of the sky,*
> *That I may fold it round me and in comfort lie.*

This is a complete poem. The other is part of a much longer poem:

> *There shut up in his castle, Tairiran's,*
> *She who had nor ears nor tongue save in her hands,*
> *Gone – ah, gone – untouched, unreachable –*
> *She who could never live save through one person,*
> *She who could never speak save to one person,*
> *And all the rest of her a shifting change,*
> *A broken bundle of mirrors . . . –*

It is obvious that the charm of these lines could not be, without the constant suggestion and the skilful evasion of iambic pentameter.

At the beginning of the seventeenth century, and especially in the verse of John Webster, who was in some ways a more cunning technician than Shakespeare, one finds the same constant evasion and recognition of regularity. Webster is much freer than Shakespeare, and that his fault is not negligence is evidenced by the fact that it is often at moments of the highest intensity that his verse acquires this freedom. That there is also carelessness I do not deny, but the irregularity of carelessness can be at once detected from the irregularity of deliberation. (In *The White Devil* Brachiano dying, and Cornelia mad, deliberately rupture the bonds of pentameter.)

I recover, like a spent taper, for a flash
and instantly go out.

Cover her face; mine eyes dazzle; she died young.

You have cause to love me, I did enter you in my heart
Before you would vouchsafe to call for the keys.

This is a vain poetry: but I pray you tell me
If there were proposed me, wisdom, riches, and beauty,
In three several young men, which should I choose?

These are not lines of carelessness. The irregularity is further enhanced by the use of short lines and the breaking up of lines in dialogue, which alters the quantities. And there are many lines in the drama of this time which are spoilt by regular accentuation.

I loved this woman in spite of my heart.
(The Changeling)
I would have these herbs grow up in his grave.
(The White Devil)
Whether the spirit of greatness or of woman...
(The Duchess of Malfi)

The general charge of decadence cannot be preferred. Tourneur and Shirley, who I think will be conceded to have touched nearly the bottom of the decline of tragedy, are much more regular than Webster or Middleton. Tourneur will polish off a fair line of iambics even at the cost of amputating a preposition from its substantive, and in the *Atheist's Tragedy* he has a final 'of' in two lines out of five together.

We may therefore formulate as follows: the ghost of some simple metre should lurk behind the arras in even the 'freest' verse; to advance menacingly as we doze, and withdraw as we rouse. Or, freedom is only truly freedom when it appears against the background of an artificial limitation.

Not to have perceived the simple truth that *some* artificial limitation is necessary except in moments of the first intensity is, I believe, a capital error of even so distinguished a talent as that of Mr E. L. Masters. The *Spoon River Anthology* is not material of the first intensity; it is reflective, not immediate; its author is a moralist, rather than an observer. His material is so near to the material of Crabbe that one wonders why he should have used a different form. Crabbe is, on the whole, the more intense of the two; he is keen, direct, and unsparing. His material is prosaic, not in the sense that it would have been better done in prose, but in the sense of requiring a simple and rather rigid verse-form and this Crabbe has given it. Mr Masters requires a more rigid verse-form than either of the two contemporary poets quoted above, and his epitaphs suffer from the lack of it.

So much for metre. There is no escape from metre; there is only mastery. But while there obviously is escape from rhyme, the *vers librists* are by no means the first out of the cave.

The boughs of the trees
Are twisted
By many bafflings;
Twisted are
The small-leafed boughs.

But the shadow of them
Is not the shadow of the mast head
Nor of the torn sails.

When the white dawn first
Through the rough fir-planks
Of my hut, by the chestnuts,
Up at the valley-head,
Came breaking, Goddess,
I sprang up, I threw round me
My dappled fawn-skin . . .

Except for the more human touch in the second of these extracts a hasty observer would hardly realize that the first is by a contemporary, and the second by Matthew Arnold.

I do not minimize the services of modern poets in exploiting the possibilities of rhymeless verse. They prove the strength of a Movement, the utility of a Theory. What neither Blake nor Arnold could do alone is being done in our time. 'Blank verse' is the only accepted rhymeless verse in English – the inevitable iambic pentameter. The English ear is (or was) more sensitive to the music of the verse and less dependent upon the recurrence of identical sounds in this metre than in any other. There is no campaign against rhyme. But it is possible that excessive devotion to rhyme has thickened the modern ear. The rejection of rhyme is not a leap at facility; on the contrary, it imposes a much severer strain upon the language. When the comforting echo of rhyme is removed, success or failure in the choice of words, in the sentence structure, in the order, is at once more apparent. Rhyme removed, the poet is at once held up to the standards of prose. Rhyme removed, much ethereal music leaps up from the word, music which has hitherto chirped unnoticed in the expanse of prose. Any rhyme forbidden, many Shagpats were unwigged.

And this liberation from rhyme might be as well a liberation *of* rhyme. Freed from its exacting task of supporting lame verse, it could be applied with greater effect where it is most needed. There are often passages in an unrhymed poem where rhyme is wanted for some special effect, for a sudden tightening-up, for a cumulative insistence, or for an abrupt change of mood. But formal rhymed verse will certainly not lose its place. We only need the coming of a Satirist – no man of genius is rarer – to prove that the heroic couplet has lost none of its edge since Dryden and Pope laid it down. As for the sonnet I am not so sure. But the decay of intricate formal patterns has nothing to do with the advent of *vers libre.* It had set in long before. Only in a closely-knit and homogeneous society, where many men are at work on the same problems, such a society as those which produced the Greek chorus, the Elizabethan lyric, and the Troubadour canzone, will the development of such forms ever be carried to perfection. And as for *vers libre,* we conclude that it is not defined by absence of pattern or absence of rhyme, for other verse is without these; that it is not defined by non-existence of metre, since even the *worst* verse can be scanned; and we conclude that the division between Conservative Verse and *vers libre* does not exist, for there is only good verse, bad verse, and chaos.

TRADITION AND THE INDIVIDUAL TALENT

I

In English writing we seldom speak of tradition, though we occasionally apply its name in deploring its absence. We cannot refer to 'the tradition' or to 'a tradition'; at most, we employ the adjective in saying that the poetry of So-and-so is 'traditional' or even 'too traditional'. Seldom, perhaps, does the word appear except in a phrase of censure. If otherwise, it is vaguely approbative, with the implication, as to the work approved, of some pleasing archaeological reconstruction. You can hardly make the word agreeable to English ears without this comfortable reference to the reassuring science of archaeology.

Certainly the word is not likely to appear in our appreciations of living or dead writers. Every nation, every race, has not only its own creative, but its own critical turn of mind; and is even more oblivious of the shortcomings and limitations of its critical habits than of those of its creative genius. We know, or think we know, from the enormous mass of critical writing that has appeared in the French language the critical method or habit of the French; we only conclude (we are such unconscious people) that the French are 'more critical' than we, and sometimes even plume ourselves a little with the fact, as if the French were the less spontaneous. Perhaps they are; but we might remind ourselves that criticism is as inevitable as breathing, and that we should be none the worse for articulating what passes in our minds when we read a book and feel an emotion about it, for criticizing our own minds in their work of criticism. One of the facts that might come to light in this process is our tendency to insist, when we praise a poet, upon those aspects of his work in which he least resembles anyone else. In these aspects or parts of his work we pretend to find what is individual, what is the peculiar essence of the man. We dwell with satisfaction upon the poet's difference from his predecessors, especially his immediate predecessors; we endeavour to find something that can be isolated in order to be enjoyed. Whereas if we approach a poet without this prejudice we shall often find that not only the best, but the most individual parts of his work may be those in which the dead poets, his ancestors, assert their immortality most vigorously. And I do not mean the impressionable period of adolescence, but the period of full maturity.

Yet if the only form of tradition, of handing down, consisted in following the ways of the immediate generation before us in a blind or timid adherence to its successes, 'tradition' should positively be discouraged. We have seen many such simple currents soon lost in the sand; and novelty is better than repetition. Tradition is a matter of much wider significance. It cannot be inherited, and if you want it you must obtain it by great labour. It involves, in the first place, the historical sense, which we may call nearly indispensable to anyone who would continue to be a poet beyond his twenty-fifth year; and the historical sense involves a perception, not only of the pastness of the past, but of its presence; the historical sense compels a man to write not merely with his own generation in his bones, but with a feeling that the whole of the literature of Europe from Homer and within it the whole of the literature of his own country has a simultaneous existence and composes a simultaneous order. This historical sense, which is a sense of the timeless as well as of the temporal and of the timeless and of the temporal together, is what makes a writer traditional. And it is at the same time what makes a writer most acutely conscious of his place in time, of his own contemporaneity.

No poet, no artist of any art, has his complete meaning alone. His significance, his appreciation is the appreciation of his relation to the dead poets and artists. You cannot value him alone; you must set him, for contrast and comparison, among the dead. I mean this as a principle of aesthetic, not merely historical, criticism. The necessity that he shall conform, that he shall cohere, is not onesided; what happens when a new work of art is created is something that happens simultaneously to all the works of art which preceded it. The existing monuments form an ideal order among themselves, which is modified by the introduction of the new (the really new) work of art among them. The existing order is complete before the new work arrives; for order to persist after the supervention of novelty, the *whole* existing order must be, if ever so slightly, altered; and so the relations, proportions, values of each work of art toward the whole are readjusted; and this is conformity between the old and the new. Whoever has approved this idea of order, of the form of European, of English literature will not find it preposterous that the past should be altered by the present as much as the present is directed by the past. And the poet who is aware of this will be aware of great difficulties and responsibilities.

In a peculiar sense he will be aware also that he must inevitably be judged by the standards of the past. I say judged, not amputated, by them; not judged to be as good as, or worse or better than, the dead; and certainly not judged by the canons of dead critics. It is a judgment, a comparison, in which two things are measured by each other. To conform merely would be for the new work not really to conform at all; it would not be new, and would therefore not be a work of art.

And we do not quite say that the new is more valuable because it fits in; but its fitting in is a test of its value – a test, it is true, which can only be slowly and cautiously applied, for we are none of us infallible judges of conformity. We say: it appears to conform, and is perhaps individual, or it appears individual, and may conform; but we are hardly likely to find that it is one and not the other.

To proceed to a more intelligible exposition of the relation of the poet to the past: he can neither take the past as a lump, an indiscriminate bolus, nor can he form himself wholly on one or two private admirations, nor can he form himself wholly upon one preferred period. The first course is inadmissible, the second is an important experience of youth, and the third is a pleasant and highly desirable supplement. The poet must be very conscious of the main current, which does not at all flow invariably through the most distinguished reputations. He must be quite aware of the obvious fact that art never improves, but that the material of art is never quite the same. He must be aware that the mind of Europe – the mind of his own country – a mind which he learns in time to be much more important than his own private mind – is a mind which changes, and that this change is a development which abandons nothing *en route*, which does not superannuate either Shakespeare, or Homer, or the rock drawing of the

Magdalenian draughtsmen. That this development, refinement perhaps, complication certainly, is not, from the point of view of the artist, any improvement. Perhaps not even an improvement from the point of view of the psychologist or not to the extent which we imagine; perhaps only in the end based upon a complication in economics and machinery. But the difference between the present and the past is that the conscious present is an awareness of the past in a way and to an extent which the past's awareness of itself cannot show.

Someone said: 'The dead writers are remote from us because we *know* so much more than they did'. Precisely, and they are that which we know.

I am alive to a usual objection to what is clearly part of my programme for the *métier* of poetry. The objection is that the doctrine requires a ridiculous amount of erudition (pedantry), a claim which can be rejected by appeal to the lives of poets in any pantheon. It will even be affirmed that much learning deadens or perverts poetic sensibility. While, however, we persist in believing that a poet ought to know as much as will not encroach upon his necessary receptivity and necessary laziness, it is not desirable to confine knowledge to whatever can be put into a useful shape for examinations, drawing-rooms, or the still more pretentious modes of publicity. Some can absorb knowledge, the more tardy must sweat for it. Shakespeare acquired more essential history from Plutarch than most men could from the whole British Museum. What is to be insisted upon is that the poet must develop or procure the consciousness of the past and that he should continue to develop this consciousness throughout his career.

What happens is a continual surrender of himself as he is at the moment to something which is more valuable. The progress of an artist is a continual self-sacrifice, a continual extinction of personality.

There remains to define this process of depersonalization and its relation to the sense of tradition. It is in this depersonalization that art may be said to approach the condition of science. I therefore invite you to consider, as a suggestive analogy, the action which takes place when a bit of finely filiated platinum is introduced into a chamber containing oxygen and sulphur dioxide.

II

Honest criticism and sensitive appreciation is directed not upon the poet but upon the poetry. If we attend to the confused cries of the newspaper critics and the susurrus of popular repetition that follows, we shall hear the names of poets in great numbers; if we seek not Blue-book knowledge but the enjoyment of poetry, and ask for a poem, we shall seldom find it. I have tried to point out the importance of the relation of the poem to other poems by other authors, and suggested the conception of poetry as a living whole of all the poetry that has ever been written. The other aspect of this Impersonal theory of poetry is the relation of the poem to its author. And I hinted, by an analogy, that the mind of the mature poet differs from that of the immature one not precisely in any valuation of 'personality', not being necessarily more interesting, or having 'more to say', but rather by being a more finely perfected medium in which special, or very varied, feelings are at liberty to enter into new combinations.

The analogy was that of the catalyst. When the two gases previously mentioned are mixed in the presence of a filament of platinum, they form sulphurous acid. This combination takes place only if the platinum is present; nevertheless the newly formed acid contains no trace of platinum, and the platinum itself is apparently unaffected: has remained inert, neutral, and unchanged. The mind of the poet is the shred of platinum. It may partly or exclusively operate upon the experience of the man himself; but, the more perfect the artist, the more completely separate in him will be the man who suffers and the mind which creates; the more perfectly will the mind digest and transmute the passions which are its material.

The experience, you will notice, the elements which enter the presence of the transforming catalyst, are of two kinds: emotions and feelings. The effect of a work of art upon the person who enjoys it is an experience different in kind from any experience not of art. It may be formed out of one emotion, or may be a combination of several; and various feelings, inhering for the writer in particular words or phrases or images, may be added to compose the final result. Or great poetry may be made without the direct use of any emotion whatever: composed out of feelings solely. Canto XV of the *Inferno* (Brunetto Latini) is a working up of the emotion evident in the situation; but the effect, though single as that of any work of art, is obtained by considerable complexity of detail. The last quatrain gives an image, a feeling attaching to an image, which 'came', which did not develop simply out of what precedes, but which was probably in suspension in the poet's mind until the proper combination arrived for it to add itself to. The poet's mind is in fact a receptacle for seizing and storing up numberless feelings, phrases, images, which remain there until all the particles which can unite to form a new compound are present together.

If you compare several representative passages of the greatest poetry you see how great is the variety of types of combination, and also how completely any semi-ethical criterion of 'sublimity' misses the mark.

For it is not the 'greatness', the intensity, of the emotions, the components, but the intensity of the artistic process, the pressure, so to speak, under which the fusion takes place, that counts. The episode of Paolo and Francesca employs a definite emotion, but the intensity of the poetry is something quite different from whatever intensity in the supposed experience it may give the impression of. It is no more intense, furthermore, than Canto XXVI, the voyage of Ulysses, which has not the direct dependence upon an emotion. Great variety is possible in the process of transmutation of emotion: the murder of Agamemnon, or the agony of Othello, gives an artistic effect apparently closer to a possible original than the scenes from Dante. In the *Agamemnon*, the artistic emotion approximates to the emotion of an actual spectator; in *Othello* to the emotion of the protagonist himself. But the difference between art and the event is always absolute; the combination which is the murder of Agamemnon is probably as complex as that which is the voyage of Ulysses. In either case there has been a fusion of elements. The ode of Keats contains a number of feelings which have nothing particular to do with the nightingale, but which the nightingale, partly perhaps because of its attractive name, and partly because of its reputation, served to bring together.

The point of view which I am struggling to attack is

perhaps related to the metaphysical theory of the substantial unity of the soul: for my meaning is, that the poet has, not a 'personality' to express, but a particular medium, which is only a medium and not a personality, in which impressions and experiences combine in peculiar and unexpected ways. Impressions and experiences which are important for the man may take no place in the poetry, and those which become important in the poetry may play quite a negligible part in the man, the personality.

I will quote a passage which is unfamiliar enough to be regarded with fresh attention in the light – or darkness – of these observations:

And now methinks I could e'en chide myself
For doating on her beauty, though her death
Shall be revenged after no common action.
Does the silkworm expend her yellow labours
For thee? For thee does she undo herself?
Are lordships sold to maintain ladyships
For the poor benefit of a bewildering minute?
Why does yon fellow falsify highways,
And put his life between the judge's lips,
To refine such a thing – keeps horse and men
To beat their valours for her?...

In this passage (as is evident if it is taken in its context) there is a combination of positive and negative emotions: an intensely strong attraction toward beauty and an equally intense fascination by the ugliness which is contrasted with it and which destroys it. This balance of contrasted emotion is in the dramatic situation to which the speech is pertinent, but that situation alone is inadequate to it. This is, so to speak, the structural emotion, provided by the drama. But the whole effect, the dominant tone, is due to the fact that a number of floating feelings, having an affinity to this emotion by no means superficially evident, have combined with it to give us a new art emotion.

It is not in his personal emotions, the emotions provoked by particular events in his life, that the poet is in any way remarkable or interesting. His particular emotions may be simple, or crude, or flat. The emotion in his poetry will be a very complex thing, but not with the complexity of the emotions of people who have very complex or unusual emotions in life. One error, in fact, of eccentricity in poetry is to seek for new human emotions to express; and in this search for novelty in the wrong place it discovers the perverse. The business of the poet is not to find new emotions, but to use the ordinary ones and, in working them up into poetry, to express feelings which are not in actual emotions at all. And emotions which he has never experienced will serve his turn as well as those familiar to him. Consequently, we must believe that 'emotion recollected in tranquillity' is an inexact formula. For it is neither emotion, nor recollection, nor without distortion of meaning, tranquillity. It is a concentration, and a new thing resulting from the concentration, of a very great number of experiences which to the practical and active person would not seem to be experiences at all; it is a concentration which does not happen consciously or of deliberation. These experiences are not 'recollected', and they finally unite in an atmosphere which is 'tranquil' only in that it is a passive attending upon the event. Of course this is not quite the whole story. There is a great deal, in the writing of poetry, which must be conscious and deliberate. In fact, the bad poet is usually unconscious where he ought to be conscious, and conscious where he ought to be unconscious. Both errors tend to make him 'personal'. Poetry is not a turning loose of emotion, but an escape from emotion; it is not the expression of personality, but an escape from personality. But, of course, only those who have personality and emotions know what it means to want to escape from these things.

III

ὁ δὲ νοῦς ἴσως θειότερόν τι καὶ ἀπαθές ἐστιν.

This essay proposes to halt at the frontiers of metaphysics or mysticism, and confine itself to such practical conclusions as can be applied by the responsible person interested in poetry. To divert interest from the poet to the poetry is a laudable aim: for it would conduce to a juster estimation of actual poetry, good and bad. There are many people who appreciate the expression of sincere emotion in verse, and there is a smaller number of people who can appreciate technical excellence. But very few know when there is an expression of *significant* emotion, emotion which has its life in the poem and not in the history of the poet. The emotion of art is impersonal. And the poet cannot reach this impersonality without surrendering himself wholly to the work to be done. And he is not likely to know what is to be done unless he lives in what is not merely the present, but the present moment of the past, unless he is conscious, not of what is dead, but of what is already living.

HAMLET

Few critics have ever admitted that *Hamlet* the play is the primary problem, and Hamlet the character only secondary. And Hamlet the character has had an especial temptation for that most dangerous type of critic: the critic with a mind which is naturally of the creative order, but which through some weakness in creative power exercises itself in criticism instead. These minds often find in Hamlet a vicarious existence for their own artistic realization. Such a mind had Goethe, who made of Hamlet a Werther; and such had Coleridge, who made of Hamlet a Coleridge; and probably neither of these men in writing about Hamlet remembered that his first business was to study a work of art. The kind of criticism that Goethe and Coleridge produced, in writing of Hamlet, is the most misleading kind possible. For they both possessed unquestionable critical insight, and both make their critical aberrations the more plausible by the substitution – of their own Hamlet for Shakespeare's – which their creative gift effects. We should be thankful that Walter Pater did not fix his attention on this play.

Two writers of our time, Mr J. M. Robertson and Professor Stoll of the University of Minnesota, have issued small books which can be praised for moving in the other direction. Mr Stoll performs a service in recalling to our attention the labours of the critics of the seventeenth and eighteenth centuries,[1] observing that

they knew less about psychology than more recent Hamlet critics, but they were nearer in spirit to Shakespeare's art; and as they insisted on the importance of the effect of the whole rather than on the importance of the leading character, they were nearer, in their old-fashioned way, to the secret of dramatic art in general.

Qua work of art, the work of art cannot be interpreted; there is nothing to interpret; we can only criticize it according to standards, in comparison to other works of art; and for 'interpretation' the chief task is the presentation of relevant historical facts which the reader is not assumed to know. Mr Robertson points out, very pertinently, how critics have failed in their 'interpretation' of *Hamlet* by ignoring what ought to be very obvious: that *Hamlet* is a stratification, that it represents the efforts of a series of men, each making what he could out of the work of his predecessors. The *Hamlet* of Shakespeare will appear to us very differently if, instead of treating the whole action of the

[1] I have never, by the way, seen a cogent refutation of Thomas Rymer's objections to *Othello*.

play as due to Shakespeare's design, we perceive his *Hamlet* to be superposed upon much cruder material which persists even in the final form.

We know that there was an older play by Thomas Kyd, that extraordinary dramatic (if not poetic) genius who was in all probability the author of two plays so dissimilar as the *Spanish Tragedy* and *Arden of Feversham*; and what this play was like we can guess from three clues: from the *Spanish Tragedy* itself, from the tale of Belleforest upon which Kyd's *Hamlet* must have been based, and from a version acted in Germany in Shakespeare's lifetime which bears strong evidence of having been adapted from the earlier, not from the later, play. From these three sources it is clear that in the earlier play the motive was a revenge motive simply; that the action or delay is caused, as in the *Spanish Tragedy*, solely by the difficulty of assassinating a monarch surrounded by guards; and that the 'madness' of Hamlet was feigned in order to escape suspicion, and successfully. In the final play of Shakespeare, on the other hand, there is a motive which is more important than that of revenge, and which explicitly 'blunts' the latter; the delay in revenge is unexplained on grounds of necessity or expediency; and the effect of the 'madness' is not to lull but to arouse the king's suspicion. The alteration is not complete enough, however, to be convincing. Furthermore, there are verbal parallels so close to the *Spanish Tragedy* as to leave no doubt that in places Shakespeare was merely *revising* the text of Kyd. And finally there are unexplained scenes – the Polonius-Laertes and the Polonius-Reynaldo scenes – for which there is little excuse; these scenes are not in the verse style of Kyd, and not beyond doubt in the style of Shakespeare. These Mr Robertson believes to be scenes in the original play of Kyd reworked by a third hand, perhaps Chapman, before Shakespeare touched the play. And he concludes, with very strong show of reason, that the original play of Kyd was, like certain other revenge plays, in two parts of five acts each. The upshot of Mr Robertson's examination is, we believe, irrefragable: that Shakespeare's *Hamlet*, so far as it is Shakespeare's, is a play dealing with the effect of a mother's guilt upon her son, and that Shakespeare was unable to impose this motive successfully upon the 'intractable' material of the old play.

Of the intractability there can be no doubt. So far from being Shakespeare's masterpiece, the play is most certainly an artistic failure. In several ways the play is puzzling, and disquieting as is none of the others. Of all the plays it is the longest and is possibly the one on which Shakespeare spent most pains; and yet he has left in it superfluous and inconsistent scenes which even hasty revision should have noticed. The versification is variable. Lines like

Look, the morn, in russet mantle clad,
Walks o'er the dew of yon high eastern hill,

are of the Shakespeare of *Romeo and Juliet.* The lines in Act V. Sc. ii,

Sir, in my heart there was a kind of fighting
That would not let me sleep . . .
Up from my cabin,
My sea-gown scarf'd about me, in the dark
Grop'd I to find out them: had my desire;
Finger'd their packet;

are of his quite mature. Both workmanship and thought are in an unstable position. We are surely justified in attributing the play, with that other profoundly interesting play of 'intractable' material and astonishing versification, *Measure for Measure,* to a period of crisis, after which follow the tragic successes which culminate in *Coriolanus. Coriolanus* may be not as 'interesting' as *Hamlet,* but it is, with *Antony and Cleopatra,* Shakespeare's most assured artistic success. And probably more people have thought *Hamlet* a work of art because they found it interesting, than have found it interesting because it is a work of art. It is the 'Mona Lisa' of literature.

The grounds of *Hamlet*'s failure are not immediately

obvious. Mr Robertson is undoubtedly correct in concluding that the essential emotion of the play is the feeling of a son towards a guilty mother:

> [Hamlet's] tone is that of one who has suffered tortures on the score of his mother's degradation.... The guilt of a mother is an almost intolerable motive for drama, but it had to be maintained and emphasized to supply a psychological solution, or rather a hint of one.

This, however, is by no means the whole story. It is not merely the 'guilt of a mother' that cannot be handled as Shakespeare handled the suspicion of Othello, the infatuation of Antony, or the pride of Coriolanus. The subject might conceivably have expanded into a tragedy like these, intelligible, self-complete, in the sunlight. *Hamlet*, like the sonnets, is full of some stuff that the writer could not drag to light, contemplate, or manipulate into art. And when we search for this feeling, we find it, as in the sonnets, very difficult to localize. You cannot point to it in the speeches; indeed, if you examine the two famous soliloquies you see the versification of Shakespeare, but a content which might be claimed by another, perhaps by the author of the *Revenge of Bussy d'Ambois*, Act V. Sc. i. We find Shakespeare's *Hamlet* not in the action, not in any quotations that we might select, so much as in an unmistakable tone which is unmistakably not in the earlier play.

The only way of expressing emotion in the form of art is by finding an 'objective correlative'; in other words, a set of objects, a situation, a chain of events which shall be the formula of that *particular* emotion; such that when the external facts, which must terminate in sensory experience, are given, the emotion is immediately evoked. If you examine any of Shakespeare's most successful tragedies, you will find this exact equivalence; you will find that the state of mind of Lady Macbeth walking in her sleep has been communicated to you by a skilful accumulation of imagined sensory impressions; the words of Macbeth on hearing of his wife's death strike us as if, given the sequence of events, these words were automatically released by the last event in the series. The artistic 'inevitability' lies in this complete adequacy of the external to the emotion; and this is precisely what is deficient in *Hamlet.* Hamlet (the man) is dominated by an emotion which is inexpressible, because it is in *excess* of the facts as they appear. And the supposed identity of Hamlet with his author is genuine to this point: that Hamlet's bafflement at the absence of objective equivalent to his feelings is a prolongation of the bafflement of his creator in the face of his artistic problem. Hamlet is up against the difficulty that his disgust is occasioned by his mother, but that his mother is not an adequate equivalent for it; his disgust envelops and exceeds her. It is thus a feeling which he cannot understand; he cannot objectify it, and it therefore remains to poison life and obstruct action. None of the possible actions can satisfy it; and nothing that Shakespeare can do with the plot can express Hamlet for him. And it must be noticed that the very nature of the *données* of the problem precludes objective equivalence. To have heightened the criminality of Gertrude would have been to provide the formula for a totally different emotion in Hamlet; it is just *because* her character is so negative and insignificant that she arouses in Hamlet the feeling which she is incapable of representing.

The 'madness' of Hamlet lay to Shakespeare's hand; in the earlier play a simple ruse, and to the end, we may presume, understood as a ruse by the audience. For Shakespeare it is less than madness and more than feigned. The levity of Hamlet, his repetition of phrase, his puns, are not part of a deliberate plan of dissimulation, but a form of emotional relief. In the character Hamlet it is the buffoonery of an emotion which can find no outlet in action; in the dramatist it is the buffoonery of an emotion which he cannot express in art. The intense feeling, ecstatic or terrible, without an object or exceeding its object, is something which every person of sensibility has known; it is doubtless a subject of study for pathologists. It often occurs in adolescence: the ordinary person puts these feelings to sleep, or trims down his feelings to fit the business world; the artist keeps them alive by his ability to intensify the world to his emotions. The Hamlet of Laforgue is an adolescent; the Hamlet of Shakespeare is not, he has not that explanation and excuse. We must simply admit that here Shakespeare tackled a problem which proved too much for him. Why he attempted it at all is an insoluble puzzle; under compulsion of what experience he attempted to express the inexpressibly horrible, we cannot ever know. We need a great many facts in his biography; and we should like to know whether, and when, and after or at the same time as what personal experience, he read Montaigne, II. xii, *Apologie de Raimond Sebond.* We should have, finally, to know something which is by hypothesis unknowable, for we assume it to be an experience which, in the manner indicated, exceeded the facts. We should have to understand things which Shakespeare did not understand himself.

THE PERFECT CRITIC

I

'Eriger en lois ses impressions personnelles,
c'est le grand effort d'un homme s'il est sincère.'
LETTRES À L'AMAZONE.

Coleridge was perhaps the greatest of English critics, and in a sense the last. After Coleridge we have Matthew Arnold; but Arnold – I think it will be conceded – was rather a propagandist for criticism than a critic, a popularizer rather than a creator of ideas. So long as this land remains an island (and we are no nearer the Continent than were Arnold's contemporaries) the work of Arnold will be important; it is still a bridge across the Channel, and it will always have been good sense. Since Arnold's attempt to correct his countrymen, English criticism has followed two directions. When a distinguished critic observed recently, in a newspaper article, that 'poetry is the most highly organized form of intellectual activity,' we were conscious that we were reading neither Coleridge nor Arnold. Not only have the words 'organized' and 'activity', occurring together in this phrase, that familiar vague suggestion of the scientific vocabulary which is characteristic of modern writing, but one asked questions which Coleridge and Arnold would not have permitted one to ask. How is it, for instance, that poetry is more 'highly organized' than astronomy, physics, or pure mathematics, which we imagine to be, in relation to the scientist who practises them, 'intellectual activity' of a pretty highly organized type? 'Mere strings of words,' our critic continues with felicity and truth, 'flung like dabs of paint across a blank canvas, may awaken surprise ... but have no significance whatever in the history of literature.' The phrases by which Arnold is best known may be inadequate, they may assemble more doubts than they dispel, but they usually have some meaning. And if a phrase like 'the most highly organized form of intellectual activity' is the highest organization of thought of which contemporary criticism, (in a distinguished representative, is capable, then, we conclude, modern criticism is degenerate.

The verbal disease above noticed may be reserved for diagnosis by and by. It is not a disease from which Mr Arthur Symons (for the quotation was, of course, not from Mr Symons) notably suffers. Mr Symons represents the other tendency; he is a representative of what is always called 'aesthetic criticism' or 'impressionistic criticism'. And it is this form of criticism which I propose to examine at once. Mr Symons, the critical successor of Pater, and partly of Swinburne (I fancy that the phrase 'sick or sorry' is the common property of all three), *is* the 'impressionistic critic'. He, if anyone, would be said to expose a sensitive and cultivated mind – cultivated, that is, by the accumulation of a considerable variety of impressions from all the arts and several languages – before an 'object'; and his criticism, if anyone's, would be said to exhibit to us, like the plate, the faithful record of the impressions, more numerous or more refined than our own, upon a mind more sensitive than our own. A record, we observe, which is also an interpretation, a translation; for it must itself impose impressions upon us, and these impressions are as much created as transmitted by the criticism. I do not say at once that this is Mr Symons; but it is the 'impressionistic' critic, and the impressionistic critic is supposed to be Mr Symons.

At hand is a volume which we may test.[1] Ten of these thirteen essays deal with single plays of Shakespeare, and it is therefore fair to take one of these ten as a specimen of the book:

> *Antony and Cleopatra* is the most wonderful, I think, of all Shakespeare's plays...

and Mr Symons reflects that Cleopatra is the most wonderful of all women:

[1] *Studies in Elizabethan Drama.* By Arthur Symons.

> The queen who ends the dynasty of the Ptolemies has been the star of poets, a malign star shedding baleful light, from Horace and Propertius down to Victor Hugo; and it is not to poets only...

What, we ask, is this for? as a page on Cleopatra, and on her possible origin in the dark lady of the Sonnets, unfolds itself. And we find, gradually, that this is not an essay on a work of art or a work of intellect; but that Mr Symons is living through the play as one might live it through in the theatre; recounting, commenting:

> In her last days Cleopatra touches a certain elevation ... she would die a thousand times, rather than live to be a mockery and a scorn in men's mouths ... she is a woman to the last ... so she dies ... the plays ends with a touch of grave pity...

Presented in this rather unfair way, torn apart like the leaves of an artichoke, the impressions of Mr Symons come to resemble a common type of popular literary lecture, in which the stories of plays or novels are retold, the motives of the characters set forth, and the work of art therefore made easier for the beginner. But this is not Mr Symons' reason for writing. The reason why we find a similarity between his essay and this form of education is that *Antony and Cleopatra* is a play with which we are pretty well acquainted, and of which we have, therefore, our own impressions. We can please ourselves with our own impressions of the characters and their emotions; and we do not find the impressions of another person, however sensitive, very significant. But if we can recall the time when we were ignorant of the French symbolists, and met with *The Symbolist Movement in Literature*, we remember that book as an introduction to wholly new feelings, as a revelation. After we have read Verlaine and Laforgue and Rimbaud and return to Mr Symons' book, we may find that our own impressions dissent from his. The book has not, perhaps, a permanent value for the one reader, but it has led to results of permanent importance for him.

The question is not whether Mr Symons' impressions are 'true' or 'false'. So far as you can isolate the 'impression', the pure feeling, it is, of course, neither true nor false. The point is that you never rest at the pure feeling; you react in one of two ways, or, as I believe Mr Symons does, in a mixture of the two ways. The moment you try to put the impressions into words, you either begin to analyse and construct, to 'ériger en lois', or you begin to create something else. It is significant that Swinburne, by whose poetry Mr Symons may at one time have been influenced, is one man in his poetry and a different man in his criticism; to this extent and in this respect only, that he is satisfying a different impulse; he is criticizing, expounding, arranging. You may say this is not the criticism of a critic, that it is emotional, not intellectual – though of this there are two opinions, but it is in the direction of analysis and construction, a beginning to 'ériger en lois', and not in the direction of creation. So I infer that Swinburne found an adequate outlet for the creative impulse in his poetry; and none of it was forced back and out through his critical prose. The style of the latter is essentially a prose style; and Mr Symons' prose is much more like Swinburne's poetry than it is like his prose. I imagine – though here one's thought is moving in almost complete darkness – that Mr Symons is far more disturbed, far more profoundly affected, by his reading than was Swinburne, who responded rather by a violent and immediate and comprehensive burst of admiration which may have left him internally unchanged. The disturbance in Mr Symons is almost, but not quite, to the point of creating; the reading sometimes fecundates his emotions to produce something new which is not criticism, but is not the expulsion, the ejection, the birth of creativeness.

The type is not uncommon, although Mr Symons is far superior to most of the type. Some writers are essentially of the type that reacts in excess of the stimulus, making something new out of the impressions, but suffer from a defect of vitality or an obscure obstruction which prevents nature from taking its course. Their sensibility alters the object, but never transforms it. Their reaction is that of the ordinary emotional person developed to an exceptional degree. For this ordinary emotional person, experiencing a work of art, has a mixed critical and creative reaction. It is made up of comment and opinion, and also new emotions which are vaguely applied to his own life. The sentimental person, in whom a work of art arouses all sorts of emotions which have nothing to do with that work of art whatever, but are accidents of personal association, is an incomplete artist. For in an artist these suggestions made by a work of art, which are purely personal, become fused with a multitude of other suggestions from multitudinous experience, and result in the production of a new object which is no longer purely personal, because it is a work of art itself.

It would be rash to speculate, and is perhaps impossible to determine, what is unfulfilled in Mr Symons' charming verse that overflows into his critical prose. Certainly we may say that in Swinburne's verse the circuit of impression and expression is complete; and Swinburne was therefore able, in his criticism, to be more a critic than Mr Symons. This gives us an intimation why the artist is – each within his own limitations – oftenest to be depended upon as a critic; his criticism will be criticism, and not the satisfaction of a suppressed creative wish – which, in most other persons, is apt to interfere fatally.

Before considering what the proper critical reaction of artistic sensibility is, how far criticism is 'feeling' and how far 'thought', and what sort of 'thought' is permitted, it may be instructive to prod a little into that other temperament, so different from Mr Symons', which issues in generalities such as that quoted near the beginning of this article.

II

'L'écrivain de style abstrait est presque toujours un sentimental, du moins un sensitif. L'écrivain artiste n'est presque jamais un sentimental, et très rarement un sensitif.'
—LE PROBLÈME DU STYLE

The statement already quoted, that 'poetry is the most highly organized form of intellectual activity,' may be taken as a specimen of the abstract style in criticism. The confused distinction which exists in most heads between 'abstract' and 'concrete' is due not so much to a manifest fact of the existence of two types of mind, an abstract and a concrete, as to the existence of another type of mind, the verbal, or philosophic. I, of course, do not imply any general condemnation of philosophy; I am, for the moment, using the word ‘philosophic’ to cover the unscientific ingredients of philosophy; to cover, in fact, the greater part of the philosophic output of the last hundred years. There are two ways in which a word may be ‘abstract’. It may have (the word ‘activity’, for example) a meaning which cannot be grasped by appeal to any of the senses; its apprehension may require a deliberate suppression of analogies of visual or muscular experience, which is none the less an effort of imagination. ‘Activity’ will mean for the trained scientist, if he employ the term, either nothing at all or something still more exact than anything it suggests to us. If we are allowed to accept certain remarks of Pascal and Mr Bertrand Russell about mathematics, we believe that the mathematician deals with objects – if he will permit us to call them objects – which directly affect his sensibility. And during a good part of history the philosopher endeavoured to deal with objects which he believed to be of the same exactness as the mathematician's. Finally Hegel arrived, and if not perhaps the first, he was certainly the most prodigious exponent of emotional systematization, dealing with his emotions as if they were definite objects which had aroused those emotions. His followers have as a rule taken for granted that words have definite meanings, overlooking the tendency of words to become indefinite emotions. (No one who had not witnessed the event could imagine the conviction in the tone of Professor Eucken as he pounded the table and exclaimed *Was ist Geist? Geist ist*...) If verbalism were confined to professional philosophers, no harm would be done. But their corruption has extended very far. Compare a mediaeval theologian or mystic, compare a seventeenth-century preacher, with any 'liberal' sermon since Schleiermacher, and you will observe that words have changed their meanings. What they have lost is definite, and what they have gained is indefinite.

The vast accumulations of knowledge – or at least of information – deposited by the nineteenth century have been responsible for an equally vast ignorance. When there is so much to be known, when there are so many fields of knowledge in which the same words are used with different meanings, when every one knows a little about a great many things, it becomes increasingly difficult for anyone to know whether he knows what he is talking about or not. And when we do not know, or when we do not know enough, we tend always to substitute emotions for thoughts. The sentence so frequently quoted in this essay will serve for an example of this process as well as any, and may be profitably contrasted with the opening phrases of the *Posterior Analytics.* Not only all knowledge, but all feeling, is in perception. The inventor of poetry as the most highly organized form of intellectual activity was not engaged in perceiving when he composed this definition; he had nothing to be aware of except his own emotion about 'poetry'. He was, in fact, absorbed in a very different 'activity' not only from that of Mr Symons, but from that of Aristotle.

Aristotle is a person who has suffered from the adherence of persons who must be regarded less as his disciples than as his sectaries. One must be firmly distrustful of accepting Aristotle in a canonical spirit; this is to lose the whole living force of him. He was primarily a man of not only remarkable but universal intelligence; and universal intelligence means that he could apply his intelligence to anything. The ordinary intelligence is good only for certain classes of objects; a brilliant man of science, if he is interested in poetry at all, may conceive grotesque judgments: like one poet because he reminds him of himself, or another because he expresses emotions which he admires; he may use art, in fact, as the outlet for the egotism which is suppressed in his own speciality. But Aristotle had none of these impure desires to satisfy; in whatever sphere of interest, he looked solely and steadfastly at the object; in his short and broken treatise he provides an eternal example – not of laws, or even of method, for there is no method except to be very intelligent, but of intelligence itself swiftly operating the analysis of sensation to the point of principle and definition.

It is far less Aristotle than Horace who has been the model for criticism up to the nineteenth century. A precept, such as Horace, or Boileau gives us, is merely an unfinished analysis. It appears as a law, a rule, because it does not appear in its most general form; it is empirical. When we understand necessity, as Spinoza knew, we are free because we assent. The dogmatic critic, who lays down a rule, who affirms a value, has left his labour incomplete. Such statements may often be justifiable as a saving of time; but in matters of great importance the critic must not coerce, and he must not make judgments of worse and better. He must simply elucidate: the reader will form the correct judgment for himself.

And again, the purely 'technical' critic – the critic, that is, who writes to expound some novelty or impart some lesson to practitioners of an art – can be called a critic only in a narrow sense. He may be analysing perceptions and the means for arousing perceptions, but his aim is limited and is not the disinterested exercise of intelligence. The narrowness of the aim makes easier the detection of the merit or feebleness of the work; even of these writers there are very few – so that their 'criticism' is of great importance within its limits. So much suffices for Campion. Dryden is far more disinterested; he displays much free intelligence; and yet even Dryden – or any *literary* critic of the seventeenth century – is not quite a free mind, compared, for instance, with such a mind as Rochefoucauld's. There is always a tendency to legislate rather than to inquire, to revise accepted laws, even to overturn, but to reconstruct out of the same material. And the free intelligence is that which is wholly devoted to inquiry.

Coleridge, again, whose natural abilities, and some of whose performances, are probably more remarkable than those of any other modern critic, cannot be estimated as an intelligence completely free. The nature of the restraint in his case is quite different from that which limited the seventeenth-century critics, and is much more personal. Coleridge's metaphysical interest was quite genuine, and was, like most metaphysical interest, an affair of his emotions. But a literary critic should have no emotions except those immediately provoked by a work of art – and these (as I have already hinted) are, when valid, perhaps not to be called emotions at all. Coleridge is apt to take leave of the data of criticism, and arouse the suspicion that he has been diverted into a metaphysical hare-and-hounds. His end does not always appear to be the return to the work of art with improved perception and intensified, because more conscious, enjoyment; his centre of interest changes, his feelings are impure. In the derogatory sense he is more 'philosophic' than Aristotle. For everything that Aristotle says illuminates the literature which is the occasion for saying it; but Coleridge only now and then. It is one more instance of the pernicious effect of emotion.

Aristotle had what is called the scientific mind – a mind which, as it is rarely found among scientists except in fragments, might better be called the intelligent mind. For there is no other intelligence than this, and so far as artists and men of letters are intelligent (we may doubt whether the level of intelligence among men of letters is as high as among men of science) their intelligence is of this kind. Sainte-Beuve was a physiologist by training; but it is probable that his mind, like that of the ordinary scientific specialist, was limited in its interest, and that this was not, primarily, an interest in art. If he was a critic, there is no doubt that he was a very good one; but we may conclude that he earned some other name. Of all modern critics, perhaps Remy de Gourmont had most of the general intelligence of Aristotle. An amateur, though an excessively able amateur, in physiology, he combined to a remarkable degree sensitiveness, erudition, sense of fact and sense of history, and generalizing power.

We assume the gift of a superior sensibility. And for sensibility wide and profound reading does not mean merely a more extended pasture. There is not merely an increase of understanding, leaving the original acute impression unchanged. The new impressions modify the impressions received from the objects already known. An impression needs to be constantly refreshed by new impressions in order that it may persist at all; it needs to take its place in a system of impressions. And this system tends to become articulate in a generalized statement of literary beauty.

There are, for instance, many scattered lines and tercets in the *Divine Comedy* which are capable of transporting even a quite uninitiated reader, just sufficiently acquainted with the roots of the language to decipher the meaning, to an impression of overpowering beauty. This impression may be so deep that no subsequent study and understanding will intensify it. But at this point the impression is emotional; the reader in the ignorance which we postulate is unable to distinguish the poetry from an emotional state aroused in himself by the poetry, a state which may be merely an indulgence of his own emotions. The poetry may be an accidental stimulus. The end of the enjoyment of poetry is a pure contemplation from which all the accidents of personal emotion are removed; thus we aim to see the object as it really is and find a meaning for the words of Arnold. And without a labour which is largely a labour of the intelligence, we are unable to attain that stage of vision *amor intellectualis Dei.*

Such considerations, cast in this general form, may appear commonplaces. But I believe that it is always opportune to call attention to the torpid superstition that appreciation is one thing, and 'intellectual' criticism something else. Appreciation in popular psychology is one faculty, and criticism another, an arid cleverness building theoretical scaffolds upon one's own perceptions or those of others. On the contrary, the true generalization is not something superposed upon an accumulation of perceptions; the perceptions do not, in a really appreciative mind, accumulate as a mass, but form themselves as a structure; and criticism is the statement in language of this structure; it is a development of sensibility. The bad criticism, on the other hand, is that which is nothing but an expression of emotion. And emotional people – such as stockbrokers, politicians, men of science – and a few people who pride themselves on being unemotional – detest or applaud great writers such as Spinoza or Stendhal because of their 'frigidity'.

The writer of the present essay once committed himself to the statement that 'The poetic critic is criticizing poetry in order to create poetry.' He is now inclined to believe that the 'historical' and the 'philosophical' critics had better be called historians and philosophers quite simply. As for the rest, there are merely various degrees of intelligence. It is fatuous to say that criticism is for the sake of 'creation' or creation for the sake of criticism. It is also fatuous to assume that there are ages of criticism and ages of creativeness, as if by plunging ourselves into intellectual darkness we were in better hopes of finding spiritual light. The two directions of sensibility are complementary; and as sensibility is rare, unpopular, and desirable, it is to be expected that the critic and the creative artist should frequently be the same person.

THE METAPHYSICAL POETS

By collecting these poems[1] from the work of a generation more often named than read, and more often read than profitably studied, Professor Grierson has rendered a service of some importance. Certainly the reader will meet with many poems already preserved in other anthologies, at the same time that he discovers poems such as those of Aurelian Townshend or Lord Herbert of Cherbury here included. But the function of such an anthology as this is neither that of Professor Saintsbury's admirable edition of Caroline poets nor that of the *Oxford Book of English Verse.* Mr Grierson's book is in itself a piece of criticism, and a provocation of criticism; and we think that he was right in including so many poems of Donne, elsewhere (though not in many editions) accessible, as documents in the case of 'metaphysical poetry'. The phrase has long done duty as a term of abuse, or as the label of a quaint and pleasant taste. The question is to what extent the so-called metaphysicals formed a school (in our own time we should say a 'movement'), and how far this so-called school

[1] *Metaphysical Lyrics and Poems of the Seventeenth Century:* Donne to Butler. Selected and edited, with an Essay, by Herbert J. C. Grierson (Oxford: Clarendon Press, London: Milford).

or movement is a digression from the main current.

Not only is it extremely difficult to define metaphysical poetry, but difficult to decide what poets practise it and in which of their verses. The poetry of Donne (to whom Marvell and Bishop King are sometimes nearer than any of the other authors) is late Elizabethan, its feeling often very close to that of Chapman. The 'courtly' poetry is derivative from Jonson, who borrowed liberally from the Latin; it expires in the next century with the sentiment and witticism of Prior. There is finally the devotional verse of Herbert, Vaughan, and Crashaw (echoed long after by Christina Rossetti and Francis Thompson); Crashaw, sometimes more profound and less sectarian than the others, has a quality which returns through the Elizabethan period to the early Italians. It is difficult to find any precise use of metaphor, simile, or other conceit, which is common to all the poets and at the same time important enough as an element of style to isolate these poets as a group. Donne, and often Cowley, employ a device which is sometimes considered characteristically 'metaphysical'; the elaboration (contrasted with the condensation) of a figure of speech to the furthest stage to which ingenuity can carry it. Thus Cowley develops the commonplace comparison of the world to a chess-board through long stanzas (*To Destiny*), and Donne, with more grace, in *A Valediction*, the comparison of two lovers to a pair of compasses. But elsewhere we find, instead of the mere explication of the content of a comparison, a development by rapid association of thought which requires considerable agility on the part of the reader.

On a round ball
A workeman that hath copies by, can lay
An Europe, Afrique, and an Asia,
And quickly make that, which was nothing, All,
So doth each teare,
Which thee doth weare,
A globe, yea world by that impression grow,
Till thy tears mixt with mine doe overflow
This world, by waters sent from thee, my heaven
dissolved so.

Here we find at least two connections which are not implicit in the first figure, but are forced upon it by the poet: from the geographer's globe to the tear, and the tear to the deluge. On the other hand, some of Donne's most successful and characteristic effects are secured by brief words and sudden contrasts:

A bracelet of bright hair about the bone,

where the most powerful effect is produced by the sudden contrast of associations of 'bright hair' and of 'bone'. This telescoping of images and multiplied associations is characteristic of the phrase of some of the dramatists of the period which Donne knew: not to mention Shakespeare, it is frequent in Middleton, Webster, and Tourneur, and is one of the sources of the vitality of their language.

Johnson, who employed the term 'metaphysical poets', apparently having Donne, Cleveland, and Cowley chiefly in mind, remarks of them that 'the most heterogeneous ideas are yoked by violence together'. The force of this impeachment lies in the failure of the conjunction, the fact that often the ideas are yoked but not united; and if we are to judge of styles of poetry by their abuse, enough examples may be found in Cleveland to justify Johnson's condemnation. But a degree of heterogeneity of material compelled into unity by the operation of the poet's mind is omnipresent in poetry. We need not select for illustration such a line as:

Notre âme est un trois-mâts cherchant son Icarie;

we may find it in some of the best lines of Johnson himself (*The Vanity of Human Wishes*):

His fate was destined to a barren strand,
A petty fortress, and a dubious hand;
He left a name at which the world grew pale,
To point a moral, or adorn a tale.

where the effect is due to a contrast of ideas, different in degree but the same in principle, as that which Johnson mildly reprehended. And in one of the finest poems of the age (a poem which could not have been written in any other age), the *Exequy* of Bishop King, the extended comparison is used with perfect success: the idea and the simile become one, in the passage in which the Bishop illustrates his impatience to see his dead wife, under the figure of a journey:

Stay for me there; I will not faile
To meet thee in that hollow Vale.
And think not much of my delay;
I am already on the way,
And follow thee with all the speed
Desire can make, or sorrows breed.
Each minute is a short degree,
And ev'ry houre a step towards thee.
At night when I betake to rest,
Next morn I rise nearer my West
Of life, almost by eight houres sail,
Than when sleep breath'd his drowsy gale. . . .
But heark! My Pulse, like a soft Drum
Beats my approach, tells Thee *I come;*
And slow howere my marches be,
I shall at last sit down by Thee.

(In the last few lines there is that effect of terror which is several times attained by one of Bishop King's admirers, Edgar Poe.) Again, we may justly take these quatrains from Lord Herbert's Ode, stanzas which would, we think, be immediately pronounced to be of the metaphysical school:

So when from hence we shall be gone,
And be no more, nor you, nor I,
As one another's mystery,
Each shall be both, yet both but one.

This said, in her up-lifted face,
Her eyes, which did that beauty crown,
Were like two starrs, that having faln down,
Look up again to find their place:

While such a moveless silent peace
Did seize on their becalmed sense,
One would have thought some influence
Their ravished spirits did possess.

There is nothing in these lines (with the possible exception of the stars, a simile not at once grasped, but lovely and justified) which fits Johnson's general observations on the metaphysical poets in his essay on Cowley. A good deal resides in the richness of association which is at the same time borrowed from and given to the word 'becalmed'; but the meaning is clear, the language simple and elegant. It is to be observed that the language of these poets is as a rule simple and pure; in the verse of George Herbert this simplicity is carried as far as it can go – a simplicity emulated without success by numerous modern poets. The *structure* of the sentences, on the other hand, is sometimes far from simple, but this is not a vice; it is a fidelity to thought and feeling. The effect, at its best, is far less artificial than that of an ode by Gray. And as this fidelity induces variety of thought and feeling, so it induces variety of music. We doubt whether, in the eighteenth century, could be found two poems in nominally the same metre, so dissimilar as Marvell's *Coy Mistress* and Crashaw's *Saint Teresa*; the one producing an effect of great speed by the use of short syllables, and the other an ecclesiastical solemnity by the use of long ones:

Love thou art absolute sole lord
Of life and death.

If so shrewd and sensitive (though so limited) a critic as Johnson failed to define metaphysical poetry by its faults, it is worth while to inquire whether we may not have more success by adopting the opposite method: by assuming that the poets of the seventeenth century (up to the Revolution) were the direct and normal development of the precedent age; and, without prejudicing their case by the adjective 'metaphysical', consider whether their virtue was not something permanently valuable, which subsequently disappeared, but ought not to have disappeared. Johnson has hit, perhaps by accident, on one of their peculiarities, when he observed that 'their attempts were always analytic'; he would not agree that, after the dissociation, they put the material together again in a new unity.

It is certain that the dramatic verse of the later Elizabethan and early Jacobean poets expresses a degree of development of sensibility which is not found in any of the prose, good as it often is. If we except Marlowe, a man of prodigious intelligence, these dramatists were directly or indirectly (it is at least a tenable theory) affected by Montaigne. Even if we except also Jonson and Chapman, these two were notably erudite, and were notably men who incorporated their erudition into their sensibility: their mode of feeling was directly and freshly altered by their reading and thought. In Chapman especially there is a direct sensuous apprehension of thought, or a recreation of thought into feeling, which is exactly what we find in Donne:

in this one thing, all the discipline
Of manners and of manhood is contained;

A man to join himself with th' Universe
In his main sway, and make in all things fit
One with that All, and go on, round as it;
Not plucking from the whole his wretched part
And into straits, or into nought revert,
Wishing the complete Universe might be
Subject to such a rag of it as he;
But to consider great Necessity.

We compare this with some modern passage:

No, when the fight begins within himself,
A man's worth something. God stoops o'er his head,
Satan looks up between his feet – both tug –
He's left, himself, i' the middle; the soul wakes
And grows. Prolong that battle through his life!

It is perhaps somewhat less fair, though very tempting as both poets are concerned with the perpetuation of love by offspring, to compare with the stanzas already quoted from Lord Herbert's Ode the following from Tennyson:

One walked between his wife and child,
With measured footfall firm and mild,
And now and then he gravely smiled.
The prudent partner of his blood

Leaned on him, faithful, gentle, good
Wearing the rose of womanhood.
And in their double love secure,
The little maiden walked demure,
Pacing with downward eyelids pure.
These three made unity so sweet,
My frozen heart began to beat,
Remembering its ancient heat.

The difference is not a simple difference of degree between poets. It is something which had happened to the mind of England between the time of Donne or Lord Herbert of Cherbury and the time of Tennyson and Browning; it is the difference between the intellectual poet and the reflective poet. Tennyson and Browning are poets, and they think; but they do not feel their thought as immediately as the odour of a rose. A thought to Donne was an experience; it modified his sensibility. When a poet's mind is perfectly equipped for its work, it is constantly amalgamating disparate experience; the ordinary man's experience is chaotic, irregular, fragmentary. The latter falls in love, or reads Spinoza, and these two experiences have nothing to do with each other, or with the noise of the typewriter or the smell of cooking; in the mind of the poet these experiences are always forming new wholes.

We may express the difference by the following

theory: The poets of the seventeenth century, the successors of the dramatists of the sixteenth, possessed a mechanism of sensibility which could devour any kind of experience. They are simple, artificial, difficult, or fantastic, as their predecessors were; no less nor more than Dante, Guido Cavalcanti, Guinicelli, or Cino. In the seventeenth century a dissociation of sensibility set in, from which we have never recovered; and this dissociation, as is natural, was aggravated by the influence of the two most powerful poets of the century, Milton and Dryden. Each of these men performed certain poetic functions so magnificently well that the magnitude of the effect concealed the absence of others. The language went on and in some respects improved; the best verse of Collins, Gray, Johnson, and even Goldsmith satisfies some of our fastidious demands better than that of Donne or Marvell or King. But while the language became more refined, the feeling became more crude. The feeling, the sensibility, expressed in the *Country Churchyard* (to say nothing of Tennyson and Browning) is cruder than that in the *Coy Mistress.*

The second effect of the influence of Milton and Dryden followed from the first, and was therefore slow in manifestation. The sentimental age began early in the eighteenth century, and continued. The poets revolted against the ratiocinative, the descriptive; they thought and felt by fits, unbalanced; they reflected. In one or two passages of Shelley's *Triumph of Life*, in the second *Hyperion* there are traces of a struggle toward unification of sensibility. But Keats and Shelley died, and Tennyson and Browning ruminated.

After this brief exposition of a theory – too brief, perhaps, to carry conviction – we may ask, what would have been the fate of the 'metaphysical' had the current of poetry descended in a direct line from them, as it descended in a direct line to them? They would not, certainly, be classified as metaphysical. The possible interests of a poet are unlimited; the more intelligent he is the better; the more intelligent he is the more likely that he will have interests: our only condition is that he turn them into poetry, and not merely meditate on them poetically. A philosophical theory which has entered into poetry is established, for its truth or falsity in one sense ceases to matter, and its truth in another sense is proved. The poets in question have, like other poets, various faults. But they were, at best, engaged in the task of trying to find the verbal equivalent for states of mind and feeling. And this means both that they are more mature, and that they wear better, than later poets of certainly not less literary ability.

It is not a permanent necessity that poets should be interested in philosophy, or in any other subject. We can only say that it appears likely that poets in our civilization, as it exists at present, must be *difficult*. Our civilization comprehends great variety and complexity, and this variety and complexity, playing upon a refined sensibility, must produce various and complex results. The poet must become more and more comprehensive, more allusive, more indirect, in order to force, to dislocate if necessary, language into his meaning. (A brilliant and extreme statement of this view, with which it is not requisite to associate oneself, is that of M. Jean Epstein, *La Poésie d'aujourd-hui*.) Hence we get something which looks very much like the conceit – we get, in fact, a method curiously similar to that of the 'metaphysical poets', similar also in its use of obscure words and of simple phrasing.

O géraniums diaphanes, guerroyeurs sortilèges,
Sacrilèges monomanes!
Emballages, dévergondages, douches! O pressoirs
Des vendanges des grands soirs!
Layettes aux abois,
Thyrses au fond des bois!
Transfusions, représailles,
Relevailles, compresses et l'éternal potion,
Angélus! n'en pouvoir plus
De débâcles nuptiales! de débâcles nuptiales!

The same poet could write also simply:

Elle est bien loin, elle pleure,
Le grand vent se lamente aussi…

Jules Laforgue, and Tristan Corbière in many of his poems, are nearer to the 'school of Donne' than any modern English poet. But poets more classical than they have the same essential quality of transmuting ideas into sensations, of transforming an observation into a state of mind.

Pour l'enfant, amoureux de cartes et d'estampes,
L'univers est égal à son vaste appétit.
Ah, que le monde est grand à la clarté des lampes!
Aux yeux du souvenir que le monde est petit!

In French literature the great master of the seventeenth century – Racine – and the great master of the nineteenth – Baudelaire – are in some ways more like each other than they are like anyone else. The greatest two masters of diction are also the greatest two psychologists, the most curious explorers of the soul. It is interesting to speculate whether it is not a misfortune that two of the greatest masters of diction in our language, Milton and Dryden, triumph with a dazzling disregard of the soul. If we continued to produce

Miltons and Drydens it might not so much matter, but as things are it is a pity that English poetry has remained so incomplete. Those who object to the 'artificiality' of Milton or Dryden sometimes tell us to 'look into our hearts and write'. But that is not looking deep enough; Racine or Donne looked into a good deal more than the heart. One must look into the cerebral cortex, the nervous system, and the digestive tracts.

May we not conclude, then, that Donne, Crashaw, Vaughan, Herbert and Lord Herbert, Marvell, King, Cowley at his best, are in the direct current of English poetry, and that their faults should be reprimanded by this standard rather than coddled by antiquarian affection? They have been enough praised in terms which are implicit limitations because they are 'metaphysical' or 'witty', 'quaint' or 'obscure', though at their best they have not these attributes more than other serious poets. On the other hand, we must not reject the criticism of Johnson (a dangerous person to disagree with) without having mastered it, without having assimilated the Johnsonian canons of taste. In reading the celebrated passage in his essay on Cowley we must remember that by wit he clearly means something more serious than we usually mean today; in his criticism of their versification we must remember in what a narrow discipline he was trained, but also how well trained; we must remember that Johnson tortures chiefly the chief offenders, Cowley and Cleveland. It would be a fruitful work, and one requiring a substantial book, to break up the classification of Johnson (for there has been none since) and exhibit these poets in all their difference of kind and of degree, from the massive music of Donne to the faint, pleasing tinkle of Aurelian Townshend – whose *Dialogue between a Pilgrim and Time* is one of the few regrettable omissions from the excellent anthology of Professor Grierson.

THE FUNCTION OF CRITICISM

I

Writing several years ago on the subject of the relation of the new to the old in art, I formulated a view to which I still adhere, in sentences which I take the liberty of quoting, because the present paper is an application of the principle they express:

'The existing monuments form an ideal order among themselves, which is modified by the introduction of the new (the really new) work of art among them. The existing order is complete before the new work arrives; for order to persist after the supervention of novelty, the *whole* existing order must be, if ever so slightly, altered; and so the relations, proportions, values of each work of art toward the whole are readjusted; and this is conformity between the old and the new. Whoever has approved this idea of order, of the form of European, of English literature will not find it preposterous that the past should be altered by the present as much as the present is directed by the past.'

I was dealing then with the artist, and the sense of tradition which, it seemed to me, the artist should have; but it was generally a problem of order; and the function of criticism seems to be essentially a problem of order too. I thought of literature then, as I think of it now, of the literature of the world, of the literature of Europe, of the literature of a single country, not as a collection of the writings of individuals, but as 'organic wholes', as systems in relation to which, and only in relation to which, individual works of literary art, and the works of individual artists, have their significance. There is accordingly something outside of the artist to which he owes allegiance, a devotion to which he must surrender and sacrifice himself in order to earn and to obtain his unique position. A common inheritance and a common cause unite artists consciously or unconsciously: it must be admitted that the union is mostly unconscious. Between the true artists of any time there is, I believe, an unconscious community. And, as our instincts of tidiness imperatively command us not to leave to the haphazard of unconsciousness what we can attempt to do consciously, we are forced to conclude that what happens unconsciously we could bring about, and form into a purpose, if we made a conscious attempt. The second-rate artist, of course, cannot afford to surrender himself to any common action; for his chief task is the assertion of all the trifling differences which are his distinction: only the man who has so much to give that he can forget himself in his work can afford to collaborate, to exchange, to contribute.

If such views are held about art, it follows that *a fortiori* whoever holds them must hold similar views about criticism. When I say criticism, I mean of course in this place the commentation and exposition of works of art by means of written words; for of the general use of the word 'criticism' to mean such writings, as Matthew Arnold uses it in his essay, I shall presently make several qualifications. No exponent of criticism (in this limited sense) has, I presume, ever made the preposterous assumption that criticism is an autotelic activity. I do not deny that art may be affirmed to serve ends beyond itself; but art is not required to be aware of these ends, and indeed performs its function, whatever that may be, according to various theories of value, much better by indifference to them. Criticism, on the other hand, must always profess an end in view, which, roughly speaking, appears to be the elucidation of works of art and the correction of taste. The critic's task, therefore, appears to be quite clearly cut out for him; and it ought to be comparatively easy to decide whether he performs it satisfactorily, and in general, what kinds of criticism are useful and what are otiose. But on giving the matter a little attention, we perceive that criticism, far from being a simple and orderly field of beneficent activity, from which impostors can be readily ejected, is no better than a Sunday park of contending and contentious orators, who have not even arrived at the articulation of their differences. Here, one would suppose, was a place for quiet cooperative labour. The critic, one would suppose, if he is to justify his existence, should endeavour to discipline his personal prejudices and cranks – tares to which we are all subject – and compose his differences with as many of his fellows as possible, in the common pursuit of true judgment. When we find that quite the contrary prevails, we begin to suspect that the critic owes his livelihood to the violence and extremity of his opposition to other critics, or else to some trifling oddities of his own with which he contrives to season the opinions which men already hold, and which out of vanity or sloth they prefer to maintain. We are tempted to expel the lot.

Immediately after such an eviction, or as soon as relief has abated our rage, we are compelled to admit that there remain certain books, certain essays, certain sentences, certain men, who have been 'useful' to us. And our next step is to attempt to classify these, and find out whether we establish any principles for deciding what kinds of book should be preserved, and what aims and methods of criticism should be followed.

II

The view of the relation of the work of art to art, of the work of literature to literature, of 'criticism' to criticism, which I have outlined above, seemed to me natural and self-evident. I owe to Mr Middleton Murry my perception of the contentious character of the problem; or rather, my perception that there is a definite and final choice involved. To Mr Murry I feel an increasing debt of gratitude. Most of our critics are occupied in labour of obnubilation; in reconciling, in hushing up, in patting down, in squeezing in, in glozing over, in concocting pleasant sedatives, in pretending that the only difference between themselves and others is that they are nice men and the others of very doubtful repute. Mr Murry is not one of these. He is aware that there are definite positions to be taken, and that now and then one must actually reject something and select something else. He is not the anonymous writer who in a literary paper several years ago asserted that Romanticism and Classicism are much the same thing, and that the true Classical Age in France was the Age which produced the Gothic cathedrals and – Jeanne d'Arc. With Mr Murry's formulation of Classicism and Romanticism I cannot agree; the difference seems to me rather the difference between the complete and the fragmentary, the adult and the immature, the orderly and the chaotic. But what Mr Murry does show is that there are at least two attitudes toward literature and toward everything, and that you cannot hold both. And the attitude which he professes appears to imply that the other has no standing in England whatever. For it is made a national, a racial issue.

Mr Murry makes his issue perfectly clear. 'Catholicism', he says, 'stands for the principle of unquestioned spiritual authority outside the individual; that is also the principle of Classicism in literature.' Within the orbit within which Mr Murry's discussion moves, this seems to me an unimpeachable definition, though it is of course not all that there is to be said about either Catholicism or Classicism. Those of us who find ourselves supporting what Mr Murry calls Classicism believe that men cannot get on without giving allegiance to something outside themselves. I am aware that 'outside' and 'inside' are terms which provide unlimited opportunity for quibbling, and that no psychologist would tolerate a discussion which shuffled such base coinage; but I will presume that Mr Murry and myself can agree that for our purpose these counters are adequate, and concur in disregarding the admonitions of our psychological friends. If you find that you have to imagine it as outside, then it is outside. If, then, a man's interest is political, he must, I presume, profess an allegiance to principles, or to a form of government, or to a monarch; and if he is interested in religion, and has one, to a Church; and if he happens to be interested in literature, he must acknowledge, it seems to me, just that sort of allegiance which I endeavoured to put forth in the preceding section. There is, nevertheless, an alternative, which Mr Murry has expressed. 'The English writer, the English divine, the English statesman, inherit no rules from their forebears; they inherit only this: a sense that in the last resort they must depend upon the inner voice.' This statement does, I admit, appear to cover certain cases; it throws a flood of light upon Mr Lloyd George. But why '*in the last resort*'? Do they, then, avoid the dictates of the inner voice up to the last extremity? My belief is that those who possess this inner voice are ready enough to hearken to it, and will hear no other. The inner voice, in fact, sounds remarkably like an old principle which has been formulated by an elder critic in the now familiar phrase of 'doing as one likes'. The possessors of the inner voice ride ten in a compartment to a football match at Swansea, listening to the inner voice, which breathes the eternal message of vanity, fear, and lust.

Mr Murry will say, with some show of justice, that this is a wilful misrepresentation. He says: 'If they (the English writer, divine, statesman) dig *deep enough* in their pursuit of self-knowledge – a piece of mining done not with the intellect alone, but with the whole man – they will come upon a self that is universal' – an exercise far beyond the strength of our football enthusiasts. It is an exercise, however, which I believe was of enough interest to Catholicism for several handbooks to be written on its practice. But the Catholic practitioners were, I believe, with the possible exception of certain heretics, not palpitating Narcissi; the Catholic did not believe that God and himself were identical. 'The man who truly interrogates himself will ultimately hear the voice of God', Mr Murry says. In theory, this leads to a form of pantheism which I maintain is not European – just as Mr Murry maintains that 'Classicism' is not English. For its practical results, one may refer to the verses of *Hudibras*.

I did not realize that Mr Murry was the spokesman for a considerable sect, until I read in the editorial columns of a dignified daily that 'magnificent as the representatives of the classical genius have been in England, they are not the sole expressions of the English character, which remains at bottom obstinately "humorous" and nonconformist'. This writer is moderate in using the qualification *sole*, and brutally frank in attributing this 'humorousness' to 'the unreclaimed Teutonic element in us'. But it strikes me that Mr Murry, and this other voice, are either too obstinate or too tolerant. The question is, the first question, *not* what comes natural or what comes *easy* to us, but what is right? Either one attitude is better than the other, or else it is indifferent. But how can such a choice be indifferent? Surely the reference to racial origins, or the mere statement that the French are thus, and the English otherwise, is not expected to settle the question: which, of two antithetical views, is *right*? And I cannot understand why the opposition between Classicism and Romanticism should be profound enough in Latin countries (Mr Murry says it is) and yet of no significance among ourselves. For if the French are *naturally* classical, why should there be any 'opposition' in France, any more than there is here? And if Classicism is not natural to them, but something acquired, why not acquire it here? Were the French in the year 1600 classical, and the English in the same year romantic? A more important difference, to my mind, is that the French in the year 1600 *had already a more mature prose.*

III

This discussion may seem to have led us a long way from the subject of this paper. But it was worth my while to follow Mr Murry's comparison of Outside Authority with the Inner Voice. For to those who obey the inner voice (perhaps 'obey' is not the word) nothing that I can say about criticism will have the slightest value. For they will not be interested in the attempt to find any common principles for the pursuit of criticism. Why have principles, when one has the inner voice? If I like a thing, that is all I want; and if enough of us, shouting all together, like it, that should be all that *you* (who don't like it) ought to want. The law of art, said Mr Clutton Brock, is all case law. And we can not only like whatever we like to like but we can like it for any reason we choose. We are not, in fact, concerned with literary *perfection* at all – the search for perfection is a sign of pettiness, for it shows that the writer has admitted the existence of an unquestioned spiritual authority outside himself, to which he has attempted to *conform*. We are not in fact interested in art. We will not worship Baal. 'The principle of classical leadership, is that obeisance is made to the office or to the tradition, never to the man.' And we want, not principles, but men.

Thus speaks the Inner Voice. It is a voice to which, for convenience, we may give a name: and the name I suggest is Whiggery.

IV

Leaving, then, those whose calling and election are sure and returning to those who shamefully depend upon tradition and the accumulated wisdom of time, and restricting the discussion to those who sympathize with each other in this frailty, we may comment for a moment upon the use of the terms 'critical' and 'creative' by one whose place, on the whole, is with the weaker brethren. Matthew Arnold distinguishes far too bluntly, it seems to me, between the two activities: he overlooks the capital importance of criticism in the work of creation itself. Probably, indeed, the larger part of the labour of an author in composing his work is critical labour; the labour of sifting, combining, constructing, expunging, correcting, testing: this frightful toil is as much critical as creative. I maintain even that the criticism employed by a trained and skilled writer on his own work is the most vital, the highest kind of criticism; and (as I think I have said before) that some creative writers are superior to others solely because their critical faculty is superior. There is a tendency, and I think it is a whiggery tendency, to decry this critical toil of the artist; to propound the thesis that the great artist is an unconscious artist, unconsciously inscribing on his banner the words Muddle Through. Those of us who are Inner Deaf Mutes are, however, sometimes compensated by a humble conscience, which, though without oracular expertness, counsels us to do the best we can, reminds us that our compositions ought to be as free from defects as possible (to atone for their lack of inspiration), and, in short, makes us waste a good deal of time. We are aware, too, that the critical discrimination which comes so hardly to us has in more fortunate men flashed in the very heat of creation; and we do not assume that because works have been composed without apparent critical labour, no critical labour has been done. We do not know what previous labours have prepared, or what goes on, in the way of criticism, all the time in the minds of the creators.

But this affirmation recoils upon us. If so large a part of creation is really criticism, is not a large part of what is called 'critical writing' really creative? If so, is there not creative criticism in the ordinary sense? The answer seems to be, that there is no equation. I have assumed as axiomatic that a creation, a work of art, is autotelic; and that criticism, by definition, is *about* something other than itself. Hence you cannot fuse creation with criticism as you can fuse criticism with creation. The critical activity finds its highest, its true fulfilment in a kind of union with creation in the labour of the artist.

But no writer is completely self-sufficient, and many creative writers have a critical activity which is not all discharged into their work. Some seem to require to keep their critical powers in condition for the real work by exercising them miscellaneously; others, on completing a work, need to continue the critical activity by commenting on it. There is no general rule. And as men can learn from each other, so some of these treatises have been useful to other writers. And some of them have been useful to those who were not writers.

At one time I was inclined to take the extreme position that the *only* critics worth reading were the critics who practised, and practised well, the art of which they wrote. But I had to stretch this frame to make some important inclusions; and I have since been in search of a formula which should cover everything I wished to include, even if it included more than I wanted. And the most important qualification which I have been able to find, which accounts for the peculiar importance of the criticism of practitioners, is that a critic must have a very highly developed sense of fact. This is by no means a trifling or frequent gift. And it is not one which easily wins popular commendations. The sense of fact is something very slow to develop, and its complete development means perhaps the very pinnacle of civilization. For there are so many spheres of fact to be mastered, and our outermost sphere of fact, of knowledge, of control, will be ringed with narcotic fancies in the sphere beyond. To the member of the Browning Study Circle, the discussion of poets about poetry may seem arid, technical, and limited. It is merely that the practitioners have clarified and reduced to a state of fact all the feelings that the member can only enjoy in the most nebulous form; the dry technique implies, for those who have mastered it, all that the member thrills to; only that has been made into something precise, tractable, under control. That, at all events, is one reason for the value of the practitioner's criticism – he is dealing with his facts, and he can help us to do the same.

And at every level of criticism I find the same necessity regnant. There is a large part of critical writing which consists in 'interpreting' an author, a work. This is not on the level of the Study Circle either; it occasionally happens that one person obtains an understanding of another, or a creative writer, which he can partially communicate, and which we feel to be true and illuminating. It is difficult to confirm the 'interpretation' by external evidence. To anyone who is skilled in fact on this level there will be evidence enough. But who is to prove his own skill? And for every success in this type of writing there are thousands of impostures. Instead of insight, you get a fiction. Your test is to apply it again and again to the original, with your view of the original to guide you. But there is no one to guarantee your competence, and once again we find ourselves in a dilemma.

We must ourselves decide what is useful to us and what is not; and it is quite likely that we are not competent to decide. But it is fairly certain that 'interpretation' (I am not touching upon the acrostic element in literature) is only legitimate when it is not interpretation at all, but merely putting the reader in possession of facts which he would otherwise have missed. I have had some experience of Extension lecturing, and I have found only two ways of leading any pupils to like anything with the right liking: to present them with a selection of the simpler kind of facts about a work – its conditions, its setting, its genesis – or else to spring the work on them in such a way that they were not prepared to be prejudiced against it. There were many facts to help them with Elizabethan drama: the poems of T. E. Hulme only needed to be read aloud to have immediate effect.

Comparison and analysis, I have said before, and Remy de Gourmont has said before me (a real master of fact – sometimes, I am afraid, when he moved outside of literature, a master illusionist of fact), are the chief tools of the critic. It is obvious indeed that they *are* tools, to be handled with care, and not employed in an inquiry into the number of times giraffes are mentioned in the English novel. They are not used with conspicuous success by many contemporary writers. You must know what to compare and what to analyse. The late Professor Ker had skill in the use of these tools. Comparison and analysis need only the cadavers on the table; but interpretation is always producing parts of the body from its pockets, and fixing them in place. And any book, any essay, any note in *Notes and Queries*, which produces a fact even of the lowest order about a work of art is a better piece of work than nine-tenths of the most pretentious critical journalism, in journals or in books. We assume, of course, that we are masters and not servants of facts, and that we know that the discovery of Shakespeare's laundry bills would not be of much use to us; but we must always reserve final judgment as to the futility of the research which has discovered them, in the possibility that some genius will appear who will know of a use to which to put them. Scholarship, even in its humblest forms, has its rights; we assume that we know how to use it, and how to neglect it. Of course the multiplication of critical books and essays may create, and I have seen it create, a vicious taste for reading about works of art instead of reading the works themselves, it may supply opinion instead of educating taste. But *fact* cannot corrupt taste; it can at worst gratify one taste – a taste for history, let us say, or antiquities, or biography – under the illusion that it is assisting another. The real corrupters are those who supply opinion or fancy; and Goethe and Coleridge are not guiltless – for what is Coleridge's *Hamlet*: is it an honest inquiry as far as the data permit, or is it an attempt to present Coleridge in an attractive costume?

We have not succeeded in finding such a test as anyone can apply; we have been forced to allow ingress to innumerable dull and tedious books; but we have, I think, found a test which, for those who are able to apply it, will dispose of the really vicious ones. And with this test we may return to the preliminary statement of the polity of literature and of criticism. For the kinds of critical work which we have admitted, there is the possibility of cooperative activity, with the further possibility of arriving at something outside of ourselves, which may provisionally be called truth. But if anyone complains that I have not defined truth, or fact, or reality, I can only say apologetically that it was no part of my purpose to do so, but only to find a scheme into which, whatever they are, they will fit, if they exist.

ANDREW MARVELL

The tercentenary of the former member for Hull deserves not only the celebration proposed by that favoured borough, but a little serious reflection upon his writing. That is an act of piety, which is very different from the resurrection of a deceased reputation. Marvell has stood high for some years; his best poems are not very many, and not only must be well known, from the *Golden Treasury* and the *Oxford Book of English Verse*, but must also have been enjoyed by numerous readers. His grave needs neither rose nor rue nor laurel; there is no imaginary justice to be done; we may think about him, if there be need for thinking, for our own benefit, not his. To bring the poet back to life – the great, the perennial, task of criticism – is in this case to squeeze the drops of the essence of two or three poems; even confining ourselves to these, we may find some precious liquor unknown to the present age. Not to determine rank, but to isolate this quality, is the critical labour. The fact that of all Marvell's verse, which is itself not a great quantity, the really valuable part consists of a very few poems indicates that the unknown quality of which we speak is probably a literary rather than a personal quality; or, more truly, that it is a quality of a civilization, of a traditional habit of life. A poet like Donne, or like Baudelaire or Laforgue, may almost be considered the inventor of an attitude, a system of feeling or of morals. Donne is difficult to analyse: what appears at one time a curious personal point of view may at another time appear rather the precise concentration of a kind of feeling diffused in the air about him. Donne and his shroud, the shroud and his motive for wearing it, are inseparable, but they are not the same thing. The seventeenth century sometimes seems for more than a moment to gather up and to digest into its art all the experience of the human mind which (from the same point of view) the later centuries seem to have been partly engaged in repudiating. But Donne would have been an individual at any time and place; Marvell's best verse is the product of European, that is to say Latin, culture.

Out of that high style developed from Marlowe through Jonson (for Shakespeare does not lend himself to these genealogies) the seventeenth century separated two qualities: wit and magniloquence. Neither is as simple or as apprehensible as its name seems to imply, and the two are not in practice antithetical; both are conscious and cultivated, and the mind which cultivates one may cultivate the other. The actual poetry, of Marvell, of Cowley, of Milton, and of others, is a blend in varying proportions. And we must be on guard not to employ the terms with too wide a comprehension; for like the other fluid terms with which literary criticism deals, the meaning alters with the age, and for precision we must rely to some degree upon the literacy and good taste of the reader. The wit of the Caroline poets is not the wit of Shakespeare, and it is not the wit of Dryden, the great master of contempt, or of Pope, the great master of hatred, or of Swift, the great master of disgust. What is meant is some quality which is common to the songs in *Comus* and Cowley's Anacreontics and Marvell's Horatian Ode. It is more than a technical accomplishment, or the vocabulary and syntax of an epoch; it is, what we have designated tentatively as wit, a tough reasonableness beneath the slight lyric grace. You cannot find it in Shelley or Keats or Wordsworth; you cannot find more than an echo of it in Landor; still less in Tennyson or Browning; and among contemporaries Mr Yeats is an Irishman and Mr Hardy is a modern Englishman – that is to say, Mr Hardy is without it and Mr Yeats is outside of the tradition altogether. On the other hand, as it certainly exists in Lafontaine, there is a large part of it in Gautier. And of the magniloquence, the deliberate exploitation of the possibilities of magnificence in language which Milton used and abused, there is also use and even abuse in the poetry of Baudelaire.

Wit is not a quality that we are accustomed to associate with 'Puritan' literature, with Milton or with Marvell. But if so, we are at fault partly in our conception of wit and partly in our generalizations about the Puritans. And if the wit of Dryden or of Pope is not the only kind of wit in the language the rest is not merely a little merriment or a little levity or a little impropriety or a little epigram. And, on the other hand, the sense in which a man like Marvell is a 'Puritan' is restricted. The persons who opposed Charles I and the persons who supported the Commonwealth were not all of the flock of Zeal-of-the-land Busy or the United Grand Junction Ebenezer Temperance Association. Many of them were gentlemen of the time who merely believed, with considerable show of reason, that government by a Parliament of gentlemen was better than government by a Stuart; though they were, to that extent, Liberal Practitioners, they could hardly foresee the tea-meeting and the Dissidence of Dissent. Being men of education and culture, even of travel, some of them were exposed to that spirit of the age which was coming to be the French spirit of the age. This spirit, curiously enough, was quite opposed to the tendencies latent or the forces active in Puritanism; the contest does great damage to the poetry of Milton; Marvell, an active servant of the public, but a lukewarm partisan, and a poet on a smaller scale, is far less injured by it. His line on the statue of Charles II, 'It is such a King as no chisel can amend', may be set off against his criticism of the Great Rebellion: 'Men ...

ought and might have trusted the King'. Marvell, therefore, more a man of the century than a Puritan, speaks more clearly and unequivocally with the voice of his literary age than does Milton.

This voice speaks out uncommonly strong in the *Coy Mistress.* The theme is one of the great traditional commonplaces of European literature. It is the theme of *O mistress mine,* of *Gather ye rosebuds,* of *Go, lovely rose*; it is in the savage austerity of Lucretius and the intense levity of Catullus. Where the wit of Marvell renews the theme is in the variety and order of the images. In the first of the three paragraphs Marvell plays with a fancy which begins by pleasing and leads to astonishment.

Had we but world enough and time,
This coyness, lady, were no crime,
. . . I would
Love you ten years before the Flood,
And you should, if you please, refuse
Till the conversion of the Jews;
My vegetable love should grow
Vaster than empires and more slow. . . .

We notice the high speed, the succession of concentrated images, each magnifying the original fancy. When this process has been carried to the end and summed up, the poem turns suddenly with that surprise which has been one of the most important means of poetic effect since Homer:

But at my back I always hear
Time's wingèd chariot hurrying near,
And yonder all before us lie
Deserts of vast eternity.

A whole civilization resides in these lines:

Pallida Mors æquo pulsat pede pauperum tabernas,
Regumque turris....

And not only Horace but Catullus himself:

Nobis, cum semel occidit brevis lux,
Nox est perpetua una dormienda.

The verse of Marvell has not the grand reverberation of Catullus's Latin; but the image of Marvell is certainly more comprehensive and penetrates greater depths than Horace's.

A modern poet, had he reached the height, would very likely have closed on this moral reflection. But the three strophes of Marvell's poem have something like a syllogistic relation to each other. After a close approach to the mood of Donne,

then worms shall try
That long-preserved virginity...
The grave's a fine and private place,
But none, I think, do there embrace,

the conclusion,

Let us roll all our strength and all
Our sweetness up into one ball,
And tear our pleasures with rough strife,
Thorough the iron gates of life.

It will hardly be denied that this poem contains wit; but it may not be evident that this wit forms the crescendo and diminuendo of a scale of great imaginative power. The wit is not only combined with, but fused into, the imagination. We can easily recognize a witty fancy in the successive images ('my *vegetable* love', 'till the conversion of the Jews'), but this fancy is not indulged, as it sometimes is by Cowley or Cleveland, for its own sake. It is structural decoration of a serious idea. In this it is superior to the fancy of *L'Allegro, Il Penseroso,* or the lighter and less successful poems of Keats. In fact, this alliance of levity and seriousness (by which the seriousness is intensified) is a characteristic of the sort of wit we are trying to identify. It is found in

Le squelette était invisible
Au temps heureux de l'art païen!

of Gautier, and in the *dandysme* of Baudelaire and Laforgue. It is in the poem of Catullus which has been quoted, and in the variation by Ben Jonson:

Cannot we delude the eyes
Of a few poor household spies?
'Tis no sin love's fruits to steal;
But the sweet thefts to reveal,
To be taken, to be seen,
These have crimes accounted been.

It is in Propertius and Ovid. It is a quality of a sophisticated literature; a quality which expands in English literature just at the moment before the English mind altered; it is not a quality which we should expect Puritanism to encourage. When we come to Gray and Collins, the sophistication remains only in the language, and has disappeared from the feeling. Gray and Collins were masters, but they had lost that hold on human values, that firm grasp of human experience, which is a formidable achievement of the Elizabethan and Jacobean poets. This wisdom, cynical perhaps but untired (in Shakespeare, a terrifying clairvoyance), leads toward, and is only completed by, the religious comprehension; it leads to the point of the *Ainsi tout leur a craqué dans la main* of Bouvard and Pécuchet.

The difference between imagination and fancy, in view of this poetry of wit, is a very narrow one. Obviously, an image which is immediately and unintentionally ridiculous is merely a fancy. In the poem *Upon Appleton House,* Marvell falls in with one of these undesirable images, describing the attitude of the house toward its master:

Yet thus the leaden house does sweat,
And scarce endures the master great;
But, where he comes, the swelling hall
Stirs, and the square grows spherical;

which, whatever its intention, is more absurd than it was intended to be. Marvell also falls into the even commoner error of images which are over-developed or distracting; which support nothing but their own misshapen bodies:

And now the salmon-fishers moist
Their leathern boats begin to hoist;
And, like Antipodes in shoes,
Have shod their heads in their canoes.

Of this sort of image a choice collection may be found in Johnson's *Life of Cowley.* But the images in the *Coy Mistress* are not only witty, but satisfy the elucidation of Imagination given by Coleridge:

This power ... reveals itself in the balance or reconcilement of opposite or discordant qualities: of sameness, with difference; of the general, with the concrete; the idea with the image; the individual with the representative; the sense of novelty and freshness with old and familiar objects; a more than usual state of emotion with more than usual order; judgment ever awake and steady self-possession with enthusiasm and feeling profound or vehement....

Coleridge's statement applies also to the following verses, which are selected because of their similarity, and because they illustrate the marked caesura which Marvell often introduces in a short line:

The tawny mowers enter next,
Who seem like Israelites to be
Walking on foot through a green sea....

And now the meadows fresher dyed,
Whose grass, with moister colour dashed,
Seems as green silks but newly washed....

He hangs in shades the orange bright,
Like golden lamps in a green night....

Annihilating all that's made
To a green thought in a green shade....

Had it lived long, it would have been
Lilies without, roses within.

The whole poem, from which the last of these quotations is drawn (*The Nymph and the Fawn*), is built upon a very slight foundation, and we can imagine what some of our modern practitioners of slight themes would have made of it. But we need not descend to an invidious contemporaneity to point the difference. Here are six lines from *The Nymph and the Fawn*:

I have a garden of my own,
But so with roses overgrown
And lilies, that you would it guess
To be a little wilderness;
And all the spring-time of the year
It only lovèd to be there.

And here are five lines from *The Nymph's Song to Hylas* in the *Life and Death of Jason*, by William Morris:

I know a little garden close
Set thick with lily and red rose.
Where I would wander if I might
From dewy dawn to dewy night,
And have one with me wandering.

So far the resemblance is more striking than the difference, although we might just notice the vagueness of allusion in the last line to some indefinite person, form, or phantom, compared with the more explicit reference of emotion to object which we should expect from Marvell. But in the latter part of the poem Morris divaricates widely:

Yet tottering as I am, and weak,
Still have I left a little breath
To seek within the jaws of death
An entrance to that happy place;
To seek the unforgotten face
Once seen, once kissed, once reft from me
Anigh the murmuring of the sea.

Here the resemblance, if there is any, is to the latter part of *The Coy Mistress.* As for the difference, it could not be more pronounced. The effect of Morris's charming poem depends upon the mistiness of the feeling and the vagueness of its object; the effect of Marvell's upon its bright, hard precision. And this precision is not due to the fact that Marvell is concerned with cruder or simpler or more carnal emotions. The emotion of Morris is not more refined or more spiritual; it is merely more vague: if anyone doubts whether the more refined or spiritual emotion can be precise, he should study the treatment of the varieties of discarnate emotion in the *Paradiso.* A curious result of the comparison of Morris's poem with Marvell's is that the former, though it appears to be more serious, is found to be the slighter; and Marvell's *Nymph and the Fawn,* appearing more slight, is the more serious.

So weeps the wounded balsam; so
The holy frankincense doth flow;
The brotherless Heliades
Melt in such amber tears as these.

These verses have the suggestiveness of true poetry; and the verses of Morris, which are nothing if not an attempt to suggest, really suggest nothing; and we are inclined to infer that the suggestiveness is the aura around a bright clear centre, that you cannot have the aura alone. The day-dreamy feeling of Morris is essentially a slight thing; Marvell takes a slight affair, the feeling of a girl for her pet, and gives it a connection with that inexhaustible and terrible nebula of emotion which surrounds all our exact and practical passions and mingles with them. Again, Marvell does this in a poem which, because of its formal pastoral machinery, may appear a trifling object:

CLORINDA: *Near this, a fountain's liquid bell*
Tinkles within the concave shell.
DAMON: *Might a soul bathe there and be clean,*
Or slake its drought?

where we find that a metaphor has suddenly rapt us to the image of spiritual purgation. There is here the element of *surprise*, as when Villon says:

Necessité faict gens mesprendre
Et faim saillir le loup des boys,

the surprise which Poe considered of the highest importance, and also the restraint and quietness of tone which makes the surprise possible. And in the verses of Marvell which have been quoted there is the making the familiar strange, and the strange familiar, which Coleridge attributed to good poetry.

The effort to construct a dream world, which alters English poetry so greatly in the nineteenth century, a dream world utterly different from the visionary realities of the *Vita Nuova* or of the poetry of Dante's contemporaries, is a problem of which various explanations may no doubt be found; in any case, the result makes a poet of the nineteenth century, of the same size as Marvell, a more trivial and less serious figure. Marvell is no greater personality than William Morris, but he had something much more solid behind him: he had the vast and penetrating influence of Ben Jonson. Jonson never wrote anything purer than Marvell's *Horatian Ode*; this ode has that same quality of wit which was diffused over the whole Elizabethan product and concentrated in the work of Jonson. And, as was said before, this wit which pervades the poetry of Marvell is more Latin, more refined, than anything that succeeded it. The great danger, as well as the greatest interest and excitement, of English prose and verse, compared with French, is that it permits and justifies an exaggeration of particular qualities to the exclusion of others. Dryden was great in wit, as Milton in magniloquence; but the former, by isolating this quality and making it by itself into great poetry, and the latter, by coming to dispense with it altogether, may perhaps have injured the language. In Dryden wit become almost fun, and thereby loses some contact with reality; becomes pure fun, which French wit almost never is.

> *The midwife placed her hand on his thick skull,*
> *With this prophetic blessing:* Be thou dull....

A numerous host of dreaming saints succeed,
Of the true old enthusiastic breed.

This is audacious and splendid; it belongs to satire beside which Marvell's Satires are random babbling, but it is perhaps as exaggerated as:

Oft he seems to hide his face,
But unexpectedly returns,
And to his faithful champion hath in place
Bore witness gloriously; whence Gaza mourns,
And all that band them to resist
His uncontrollable intent.

How oddly the sharp Dantesque phrase 'whence Gaza mourns' springs out from the brilliant contortions of Milton's sentence!

Who from his private gardens, where
He lived reservèd and austere,
(As if his highest plot
To plant the bergamot)

Could by industrious valour climb
To ruin the great work of Time,

And cast the kingdoms old
Into another mold;

* * *

The Pict no shelter now shall find
Within his parti-coloured mind,
But, from this valour sad,
Shrink underneath the plaid:

There is here an equipoise, a balance and proportion of tones, which, while it cannot raise Marvell to the level of Dryden or Milton, extorts an approval which these poets do not receive from us, and bestows a pleasure at least different in kind from any they can often give. It is what makes Marvell a classic; or classic in a sense in which Gray and Collins are not; for the latter, with all their accredited purity, are comparatively poor in shades of feeling to contrast and unite.

We are baffled in the attempt to translate the quality indicated by the dim and antiquated term wit into the equally unsatisfactory nomenclature of our own time. Even Cowley is only able to define it by negatives:

Comely in thousand shapes appears;
Yonder we saw it plain; and here 'tis now,
Like spirits in a place, we know not how.

It has passed out of our critical coinage altogether, and no new term has been struck to replace it; the quality seldom exists, and is never recognized.

In a true piece of Wit all things must be
Yet all things there agree;
As in the Ark, join'd without force or strife,
All creatures dwelt, all creatures that had life.
Or as the primitive forms of all
(If we compare great things with small)
Which, without discord or confusion, lie
In that strange mirror of the Deity.

So far Cowley has spoken well. But if we are to attempt even no more than Cowley, we, placed in a retrospective attitude, must risk much more than anxious generalizations. With our eye still on Marvell, we can say that wit is not erudition; it is sometimes stifled by erudition, as in much of Milton. It is not cynicism, though it has a kind of toughness which may be confused with cynicism by the tender-minded. It is confused with erudition because it belongs to an educated mind, rich in generations of experience; and it is confused with cynicism because it implies a constant inspection and criticism of experience. It involves, probably, a recognition, implicit in the expression of every experience, of other kinds of experience which are possible, which we find as clearly in the greatest as in poets like Marvell. Such a general statement may seem to take us a long way from *The Nymph and the Fawn*, or even from the *Horatian Ode*; but it is perhaps justified by the desire to account for that precise taste of Marvell's which finds for him the proper degree of seriousness for every subject which he treats. His errors of taste, when he trespasses, are not sins against this virtue; they are conceits, distended metaphors and similes, but they never consist in taking a subject too seriously or too lightly. This virtue of wit is not a peculiar quality of minor poets, or of the minor poets of one age or of one school; it is an intellectual quality which perhaps only becomes noticeable by itself, in the work of lesser poets. Furthermore, it absent from the work of Wordsworth, Shelley, and Keats, on whose poetry nineteenth-century criticism has unconsciously been based. To the best of their poetry wit is irrelevant:

> *Art thou pale for weariness*
> *Of climbing heaven and gazing on the earth,*
> *Wandering companionless*
> *Among the stars that have a different birth,*
> *And ever changing, like a joyless eye,*
> *That finds no object worth its constancy?*

We should find it difficult to draw any useful comparison between these lines of Shelley and anything by Marvell. But later poets, who would have been the better for Marvell's quality, were without it; even Browning seems oddly immature, in some way, beside Marvell. And nowadays we find occasionally good irony or satire, which lack wit's internal equilibrium, because their voices are essentially protests against some outside sentimentality or stupidity; or we find serious poets who seem afraid of acquiring wit, lest they lose intensity. The quality which Marvell had, this modest and certainly impersonal virtue – whether we call it wit or reason, or even urbanity – we have patently failed to define. By whatever name we call it, and however we define that name, it is something precious and needed and apparently extinct; it is what should preserve the reputation of Marvell. *C'était une belle âme, comme on ne fait plus à Londres.*

ULYSSES, ORDER, AND MYTH

Mr Joyce's book has been out long enough for no more general expression of praise, or expostulation with its detractors, to be necessary; and it has not been out long enough for any attempt at a complete measurement of its place and significance to be possible. All that one can usefully do at this time, and it is a great deal to do, for such a book, is to elucidate any aspect of the book – and the number of aspects is indefinite – which has not yet been fixed. I hold this book to be the most important expression which the present age has found; it is a book to which we are all indebted, and from which none of us can escape. These are postulates for anything that I have to say about it, and I have no wish to waste the reader's time by elaborating my eulogies; it has given me all the surprise, delight, and terror that I can require, and I will leave it at that.

Among all the criticisms I have seen of the book, I have seen nothing – unless we except, in its way, M. Valéry Larbaud's valuable paper which is rather an Introduction than a criticism – which seemed to me to appreciate the significance of the method employed – the parallel to the *Odyssey*, and the use of appropriate styles and symbols to each division. Yet one might expect this to be the first peculiarity to attract attention; but it has been treated as an amusing dodge, or scaffolding erected by the author for the purpose of disposing his realistic tale, of no interest in the completed structure. The criticism which Mr Aldington directed upon *Ulysses* several years ago seems to me to fail by this oversight – but, as Mr Aldington wrote before the complete work had appeared, fails more honourably than the attempts of those who had the whole book before them. Mr Aldington treated Mr Joyce as a prophet of chaos; and wailed at the flood of Dadaism which his prescient eye saw bursting forth at the tap of the magician's rod. Of course, the influence which Mr Joyce's book may have is from my point of view an irrelevance. A very great book may have a very bad influence indeed; and a mediocre book may be in the event most salutary. The next generation is responsible for its own soul; a man of genius is responsible to his peers, not to a studio full of uneducated and undisciplined coxcombs. Still, Mr Aldington's pathetic solicitude for the half-witted seems to me to carry certain implications about the nature of the book itself to which I cannot assent; and this is the important issue. He finds the book, if I understand him, to be an invitation to chaos, and an expression of feelings which are perverse, partial, and a distortion of reality. But unless I quote Mr Aldington's words I am likely to falsify. 'I say, moreover,' he says,[1] 'that when Mr Joyce,

[1] *English Review*, April, 1921.

with his marvellous gifts, uses them to disgust us with mankind, he is doing something which is false and a libel on humanity.' It is somewhat similar to the opinion of the urbane Thackeray upon Swift. 'As for the moral, I think it horrible, shameful, unmanly, blasphemous: and giant and great as this Dean is, I say we should hoot him.' (This, of the conclusion of the Voyage to the Houyhnhnms – which seems to me one of the greatest triumphs that the human soul has ever achieved. It is true that Thackeray later pays Swift one of the finest tributes that a man has ever given or received: 'So great a man he seems to me that thinking of him is like thinking of an empire falling.' And Mr Aldington, in his time, is almost equally generous.)

Whether it is possible to libel humanity (in distinction to libel in the usual sense, which is libelling an individual or a group in contrast with the rest of humanity) is a question for philosophical societies to discuss; but of course if *Ulysses* were a 'libel' it would simply be a forged document, a powerless fraud, which would never have extracted from Mr Aldington a moment's attention. I do not wish to linger over this point: the interesting question is that begged by Mr Aldington when he refers to Mr Joyce's 'great *undisciplined* talent'.

I think that Mr Aldington and I are more or less agreed as to what we want in principle, and agreed to call it classicism. It is because of this agreement that I have chosen Mr Aldington to attack on the present issue. We are agreed as to what we want, but not as to how to get it, or as to what contemporary writing exhibits a tendency in that direction. We agree, I hope, that 'classicism' is not an alternative to 'romanticism', as of political parties, Conservative and Liberal, Republican and Democrat, on a 'turn-the-rascals-out' platform. It is a goal toward which all good literature strives, so far as it is good, according to the possibilities of its place and time. One can be 'classical', in a sense, by turning away from nine-tenths of the material which lies at hand and selecting only mummified stuff from a museum – like some contemporary writers, about whom one could say some nasty things in this connection, if it were worth while (Mr Aldington is not one of them). Or one can be classical in tendency by doing the best one can with the material at hand. The confusion springs from the fact that the term is applied to literature and to the whole complex of interests and modes of behaviour and society of which literature is a part; and it has not the same bearing in both applications. It is much easier to be a classicist in literary criticism than in creative art – because in criticism you are responsible only for what you want, and in creation you are responsible for what you can do with material which you must simply accept.

And in this material I include the emotions and feelings of the writer himself, which, for that writer, are simply material which he must accept – not virtues to be enlarged or vices to be diminished. The question, then, about Mr Joyce, is: how much living material does he deal with, and how does he deal with it: deal with, not as a legislator or exhorter, but as an artist?

It is here that Mr Joyce's parallel use of the *Odyssey* has a great importance. It has the importance of a scientific discovery. No one else has built a novel upon such a foundation before: it has never before been necessary. I am not begging the question in calling *Ulysses* a 'novel'; and if you call it an epic it will not matter. If it is not a novel, that is simply because the novel is a form which will no longer serve; it is because the novel, instead of being a form, was simply the expression of an age which had not sufficiently lost all form to feel the need of something stricter. Mr Joyce has written one novel – the *Portrait*; Mr Wyndham Lewis has written one novel – *Tarr*. I do not suppose that either of them will ever write another 'novel'. The novel ended with Flaubert and with James. It is, I think, because Mr Joyce and Mr Lewis, being 'in advance' of their time, felt a conscious or probably unconscious dissatisfaction with the form, that their novels are more formless than those of a dozen clever writers who are unaware of its obsolescence.

In using the myth, in manipulating a continuous parallel between contemporaneity and antiquity, Mr Joyce is pursuing a method which others must pursue after him. They will not be imitators, any more than the scientist who uses the discoveries of an Einstein in pursuing his own, independent, further investigations. It is simply a way of controlling, of ordering, of giving a shape and a significance to the immense panorama of futility and anarchy which is contemporary history. It is a method already adumbrated by Mr Yeats, and of the need for which I believe Mr Yeats to have been the first contemporary to be conscious. It is a method for which the horoscope is auspicious. Psychology (such as it is, and whether our reaction to it be comic or serious), ethnology, and *The Golden Bough* have concurred to make possible what was impossible even a few years ago. Instead of narrative method, we may now use the mythical method. It is, I seriously believe, a step toward making the modern world possible for art, toward that order and form which Mr Aldington so earnestly desires. And only those who have won their own discipline in secret and without aid, in a world which offers very little assistance to that end, can be of any use in furthering this advance.

INDEX OF FIRST LINES